HOW TO THINK MORE AND BETTER

HOW TO THINK MORE AND BETTER

Being Reasonable in Unreasonable Times

William B. Irvine

OXFORD
UNIVERSITY PRESS

Oxford University Press is a department of the University of Oxford.
It furthers the University's objective of excellence in research, scholarship,
and education by publishing worldwide. Oxford is a registered trade mark of
Oxford University Press in the UK and certain other countries.

Published in the United States of America by Oxford University Press
198 Madison Avenue, New York, NY 10016, United States of America.

© William B. Irvine 2026

All rights reserved. No part of this publication may be reproduced, stored
in a retrieval system, transmitted, used for text and data mining, or used for
training artificial intelligence, in any form or by any means, without the prior
permission in writing of Oxford University Press, or as expressly permitted
by law, by license or under terms agreed with the appropriate reprographics
rights organization. Inquiries concerning reproduction outside the scope of
the above should be sent to the Rights Department, Oxford University Press,
at the address above.

You must not circulate this work in any other form
and you must impose this same condition on any acquirer.

CIP data is on file at the Library of Congress

ISBN 978-0-19-778684-0

DOI: 10.1093/oso/9780197786840.001.0001

Printed by Sheridan Books, Inc., United States of America

The manufacturer's authorized representative in the EU for product safety is
Oxford University Press España S.A., Parque Empresarial San Fernando de
Henares, Avenida de Castilla, 2 – 28830 Madrid (www.oup.es/en or product.
safety@oup.com). OUP España S.A. also acts as importer into Spain of products
made by the manufacturer.

To Jenny and Ryan, with much love

CONTENTS

Preface *ix*
Acknowledgments *xv*

An Invitation to Think *1*

PART I Belief, Reconsidered

1. What Does It Mean to Believe? *17*
2. Coming to Believe *29*
3. Proving and Disproving Claims *41*
4. Inconsistent Beliefs *55*

PART II Word Problems

5. Ambiguous Words *77*
6. Emotive Language *89*
7. Linguistic Pitfalls *99*

PART III Thinking Our Way Through a Complex World

8. Understanding Causation *109*
9. Solving Problems in a Complex World *127*
10. Making Decisions in a Complex World *143*

PART IV   Cognitive Biases

11. Confirmation Bias   *159*
12. What Do You Know?   *171*
13. Along Comes the Internet   *183*

PART V   Intellectual Self-Transformation

14. Mindcare   *201*
15. Mindcleaning   *211*
16. Mind Expansion   *221*
17. Portrait of a Thinker   *227*
18. Thinking 101   *235*

APPENDIX   *239*
NOTES   *243*
INDEX   *261*

PREFACE

You obviously know how to think; otherwise, you wouldn't be reading these words. There is an excellent chance, though, that like your physical fitness, your mental fitness can be improved.

Even really smart people are capable of thinking more and better. To see why I say this, consider a scientist who has been trained to draw conclusions on the basis of carefully gathered evidence. Discuss a scientific issue with him, and he will be able to explain, calmly and rationally, how he reached his conclusions. Turn the discussion to politics, though, and his temper might flare. Rather than trying to defend his views, he might dismiss those who disagree with him as being bigoted dunces. Although this scientist is clearly thoughtful, he is selective in what he thinks about. As a result, on encountering a topic outside his area of expertise, he might let his guard down. This is particularly true with respect to charged topics, like politics.

The thought processes used to draw political conclusions will, of course, differ from those used in science, but both will involve gathering evidence and reasoning our way from that evidence to conclusions. This is where the above-mentioned scientist has room for improvement. With some effort, he can become more knowledgeable about politics, political processes, and the issues of the day. On doing so, he won't have to get angry when someone challenges his conclusions; he can instead calmly, rationally defend them. The upshot is that this scientist is capable of thinking *more*—capable, that is, of devoting careful thought to a wider range of subjects.

And besides thinking more, he can probably think *better*. There is a danger, in particular, that even when drawing conclusions within his area of expertise, he will fall victim to the systematic errors in reasoning known as *cognitive biases*. He might, for example, succumb to *confirmation bias*: In his search for evidence with respect to some phenomenon, he might unconsciously seek evidence that supports his current beliefs and ignore evidence that challenges them. To avoid making such mistakes, he needs to familiarize himself with these biases and then consciously take steps to prevent them from distorting his thought processes.

In these pages, I present a thought regimen, the goal of which is to help you think more and better than you currently do. I realize that doing this might seem presumptuous: Who am I to tell others how to think? Do I take myself to be the ultimate thinker? By no means; indeed, I am acutely aware of my intellectual shortcomings—an awareness, I should add, that is essential if one is to improve one's reasoning ability. This awareness has led me to take a closer look at how we humans think, which in turn has provided me with important insights into how and why we go wrong in forming beliefs, making decisions, and dealing with problems.

The goal of my thought regimen is to help people "optimize" their mind by filling it, to the extent possible, with true and useful beliefs.[1] To accomplish this goal, I help them sharpen their critical thinking skills so they can avoid acquiring mistaken beliefs and so they can find and eradicate those that slipped past their critical guard. At the same time, I encourage them to become more open-minded so they can acquire new true beliefs.

Before moving on, let me head off some possible misconceptions. You might assume that to think more and better, you will have to extinguish your emotions, but as we shall see, this is not the case. You might also assume that my objective in these pages is to help you "win arguments" by intellectually crushing those who disagree with you. Lots of books do that, but not this one. To the contrary, I will discourage you from seeking such encounters; indeed, if you want to persuade someone, debating them is not only unlikely to change their mind but might cause them to cling even more tightly to whatever claim they are making.

If ego gratification is your goal, then by all means learn how to win arguments. But if your goal is instead to improve your mind, your time and energy are better spent having thoughtful discussions and, in particular, having discussions with people *who thoughtfully disagree with you.* There is a chance, after all, that it isn't your interlocutor who's mistaken—it's you! If this is indeed the case, conversing with other people, listening carefully to the points they make, and being open to the information and perspectives they provide can help you eradicate your mistaken beliefs and thereby bring you closer to achieving your mind-optimization goal.

Although most people acknowledge the importance of pursuing the truth, they don't make a conscious commitment to pursue it. Laziness is one obstacle. In much the same way as physical laziness can prevent you from exercising as much as you should, mental laziness can inhibit your thinking. Mind optimization, however, will require considerable thought, and to help prepare you for this intellectual undertaking, I will play the role of mental-fitness coach. As such, I will not waste time telling you what to think; I will instead help you think more and better, so you can decide for yourself what to think. Be advised, though, that in the process of doing this, I will be a demanding coach. I will ask you to think about things you haven't thought about. More annoyingly, I will ask you to rethink your current beliefs. And more annoyingly still, I will ask you to think carefully about things you would prefer not to think about at all.

Your ego is the other major obstacle to your pursuit of the truth. It has no interest in optimizing your mind, preferring instead to optimize your self-image, as well as your public image. To achieve the former objective, it conceals from you the mistakes you make in forming beliefs and subsequently acting on them, and to achieve the latter, it prods you to say and do things that make you look smart in the eyes of other people. It is perfectly willing to interfere with your thought processes to accomplish these objectives. As a result, you might find yourself unwilling to admit your ignorance with respect to a number of subjects, in which case it will be anathema for you to utter the words "I don't know." You might also be unwilling to admit that you harbor mistaken, and even contradictory beliefs. You will therefore conclude that it is a waste of time to look for them, which will dramatically decrease your chances of eradicating them.

Your ego might also prod you to dismiss other people's criticisms. If they confront you with evidence that your beliefs are mistaken, you might ignore what they say or, more aggressively, you might silence them by cutting them off mid-sentence or even by insulting them. You have doubtless detected these propensities in other people, including your relatives, friends, and co-workers.

Engage in a bit of honest introspection, though, and you will likely detect them in yourself.

Your journey toward mind-optimization will therefore be doubly challenging. Thinking rather than feeling your way to conclusions will be *mentally* challenging, and confronting your intellectual shortcomings will be *emotionally* challenging. None of us enjoys facing hard truths about ourselves, and radical changes to our beliefs can be difficult to process. Furthermore, you must embark on this journey in the realization that you will never achieve perfect optimization. Because you are only human, with limited time, energy, and resources, there will always be things you don't know and things you mistakenly believe. And because you are human, you have emotions that can interfere with your reasoning ability. You can't eliminate these emotions, and even if you could, it would be foolish to do so: Would you want to live without being able to experience delight, hope, and love? Would you, in other words, want to spend your life in a depressed state?

These days, it is easy to find individuals who are convinced of the truth of beliefs that are in fact mistaken; indeed, such people run rampant on social media. They are happy to regurgitate claims that have repeatedly been debunked and to espouse bizarre conspiracy theories. They might also reject not only specific scientific claims but science itself. Interact with them, and you will discover that these individuals are indifferent to evidence and impervious to reason. They might also resent your efforts on their behalf; indeed, they might manifest this resentment by verbally assaulting you. Such people have always been with us. In the past, though, they were limited to lecturing family members at Thanksgiving dinners; now, they can acquire followers that number in the thousands or even millions, and their influence can have a profound effect on both society and politics. Regrettably, this influence has often been detrimental.

You can't, simply by waving a wand, transform people into rational beings, but you have it in your power to add one person to the ranks of the rational. That person is you!

Learning to think more and better will have a profound impact on your life, but it can also benefit the society in which you live. Your presence can remind others that it *is* possible to think rather than feel their way to conclusions, and your willingness to calmly, dispassionately explain and defend your beliefs can remind them of the value of civil discourse. Even if you don't succeed in persuading other people, your efforts might reduce their level of confidence in their mistaken beliefs, which in turn can reduce the chance that they act on them—to their detriment, and maybe yours as well. And best of all, they might adopt the thought processes you use to think more and better about the world around you. In many cases this won't happen, but in some cases, it might. Call me a dreamer.

ACKNOWLEDGMENTS

I would like to thank Wright State University for granting me the sabbatical during which much of this book was written. And I would especially like to thank the students who, during our interactions over nearly four decades, helped me think about how to think more and better.

An Invitation to Think

I taught critical thinking to college students for decades. I initially taught my courses the way I had been taught—on the assumption that by exposing students to deductive and inductive logic, I could transform them into fully rational beings capable of reasoning their way through life. Only later, in conjunction with research I was doing on human desire,[1] did I realize that if our goal is to think rather than feel our way through life, we need to supplement our understanding of logic with an understanding of psychology and, in particular, evolutionary psychology—a field of study, I should add, that barely existed when I started college.

For present purposes, the key takeaway from evolutionary psychology is that our brain evolved not so we modern humans could carefully reason our way from evidence to conclusions, but so our ancestors could survive and reproduce on the savannas of Africa during the last few million years. Indeed, our prefrontal cortex—the part of our brain where structured reasoning primarily takes place—was an evolutionary latecomer. And when it arrived, it didn't *replace* the components responsible for our emotions, including, most significantly, those that comprise our limbic system; it instead *joined* them. As a result, we are susceptible to having our attempts to reason our way through life derailed by our emotions. Stated simply, our head can be in conflict with our heart and gut.

Along these lines, think about the last time you had a crush on someone. Your head might have been powerless to prevent your heart from pursuing its objectives. Alternatively, think about the last time you got angry. Your head ceded control of your actions to your gut: In becoming a mad man, you transmogrified, for a time, into a madman. It is also possible for your emotions to hijack your head for an extended period. Under these circumstances your head, rather than *reasoning* its way to conclusions, will spend its time and energy *rationalizing* the impulses that arise in your heart and gut.

Even when you keep your emotions at bay, your attempts to reason can go awry. On the savannas of Africa, your ancestors often needed to make snap judgments: What, for example, were the intentions of the stranger walking toward them? And what was the source of that rustling noise in the grass? As a result, evolution wired their brains to form beliefs quickly and on the basis of minimal evidence. For better or worse, we have inherited that wiring. It was only late in the twentieth century that psychologists, led by Daniel Kahneman and Amos Tversky, made a careful study of these "cognitive biases."

Because our mind isn't perfectly rational, it can fill with mistaken beliefs, in which case we will become dangerously detached from reality. Before we proceed, though, some explanation is in order.

What Is Reality?

Tell college students that it is important to stay grounded in reality and they might respond that different people have different realities, and in particular that *their* reality is different than that of their professors. The implication is that there isn't one reality in which to be grounded, meaning that it is pointless to talk about staying grounded in reality.

What these students are trying to say, I think, is that different people are *in different circumstances*, a claim that is indisputably true. On encountering such students, I would therefore explain that I was using *reality* to refer not to their "personal reality" but to the objective reality that all people share, regardless of their circumstances. In this shared reality, certain things exist—including stars, kangaroos, viruses, and even the exotic subatomic particles known as *charm quarks*—but other things don't exist, including ghosts and Bigfoot. In this reality, the world works in a certain way. Gravity, for example, attracts things with mass, but crystals lack "healing power." Likewise, certain events have taken place—we landed on the moon, Columbus sailed to the Americas, and dinosaurs went extinct—but other events haven't taken place, such as Noah building an ark and filling it with land-dwelling animals.

To be sure, the structure of objective reality is open to debate. Someone can argue, for example, that Bigfoot *does* exist, that crystals *do* have healing power, or that Noah *did* build an ark. Alternatively, someone can argue that charm quarks *don't* exist. In making such claims, though, a person isn't denying the existence of an objective reality; they are simply arguing about the details of that reality. A full-blown "reality denier" wouldn't see any point in arguing about these details, the way a Marvel Universe denier like myself doesn't see any point in arguing about whether Captain America or the Hulk would prevail in a fair fight.

Objective reality not only exists, it bites. It is ferociously uncompromising and is utterly indifferent to human suffering. It doesn't care about your desires and beliefs for the simple reason that as an inanimate thing, it is incapable of caring. You therefore ignore its existence and workings at your peril. This is particularly true if you find yourself in dire straits, since under those circumstances there will be little margin for error.

Fortunately for us, reality is terrible at keeping secrets; indeed, it incessantly supplies us with clues about its structure and workings. By looking for and studying this evidence, we gain the ability to understand the present—and more significantly, to predict the future, so we can affect what happens, which in turn can have a profound impact on our well-being. This is why it is important to stay grounded in reality, and it is why a thoughtful person will expend the intellectual effort necessary to do so. More precisely, this is why you should strive to optimize your mind by filling it, to the extent possible, with beliefs that reflect reality.[2] To acquire these beliefs, you must carefully gather and interpret evidence, and in doing so, you must be careful to guard against being led astray by the promptings of your heart and gut. You must also spend time and energy tracking down and eradicating any mistaken beliefs that slipped past your critical guard.

To optimize your mind, though, it isn't enough that you avoid false beliefs; you must also acquire new true beliefs. To see why, consider a person who is a skilled critical thinker but has a closed mind. She will likely have many true beliefs, but because her mind is closed, she will be oblivious to many others. She would therefore benefit from opening her mind. Now consider a person who lacks critical thinking skills but has a mind that is wide open. Because he doesn't screen incoming ideas, he will end up believing many true things but also many things that are not only false, but dangerously so.

By thinking critically, you reject beliefs; by being open-minded, you recruit them. This means that the goal of thinking critically is in tension with the goal of being open-minded. These two goals, however, complement each other nicely, which is why, if you wish to optimize your mind, you should strive to become *both* more open-minded *and* more skilled at critical thinking. Your goal, in other words, should be to transform yourself into an open-minded critical thinker.

The phrase "open-minded critical thinker" is unwieldy, though, so in these pages I shall refer to such individuals simply as *Thinkers*, written with an uppercase *T*. And before moving on, a word of explanation is in order. In what follows, I will typically use feminine pronouns in reference to Thinkers. I do this not because I believe that only women can be Thinkers. That obviously isn't the case. I do it because continually switching genders in reference to the archetypal Thinker can make discussions needlessly complex. I therefore decided to choose the Thinker's default gender with a toss of a coin. "She" won.

A Closer Look at Thinkers

A Thinker, in my sense of the word, isn't simply someone who thinks a lot. *Everyone* thinks a lot; indeed, during our waking hours, we are likely to be nonstop thinkers. In some cases, we consciously summon up thoughts—when, for example, we are working on a Sudoku puzzle—but most of the time thoughts simply drift into our mind, uninvited. If you don't believe me, try to empty your mind of all thought for a few minutes. Despite your efforts, you will soon lapse into thought. Some thoughts will simply drift through your mind, but others will march in and take charge. These intrusive thoughts can keep you up at night, and obsessive thoughts can take control of your life. Like it or not, your mind has a mind of its own.

To become a Thinker, in my sense of the word, it isn't enough that you commit to the goal of optimizing your mind via open-minded critical thinking; you must also make a conscious effort to achieve that goal. To better understand what this will involve, consider what it means to be a scientist. It isn't enough that you like science or even know a lot about science. It also isn't enough that you identify as a scientist. To play the role of scientist, you must actively employ what is known as the *scientific method* in deciding which scientific claims to accept and which to reject. This will involve, among other things, making careful observations, forming hypotheses based on those observations, and testing those hypotheses with further observation and maybe experimentation as well.

Much the same can be said of Thinkers. To count as one, it isn't enough that you think a lot or like to think. It also isn't enough that you identify as a Thinker. To count as a Thinker, you must routinely and consciously engage in evidence-based systematic thinking. This will include not only relying on the scientific method to determine which scientific claims to accept, but relying on other kinds of systematic thinking to form beliefs, deal with problems, and make decisions. You must also take care that your thought processes aren't undermined by your feelings. And finally, you must endeavor to keep your mind open—but not too open. In the pages that follow, I will explain, in considerable detail, how Thinkers think. My goal in doing this is to help readers think more and better than they currently do. More ambitiously, my goal is to transform them into Thinkers.

Before moving on, let me address some of the misconceptions that might arise with respect to the Thinker concept. The first is to assume that a Thinker will be anti-emotion and maybe even that her goal will be to extinguish her emotions. *This is not the case.* For one thing, a Thinker will realize that because of how she is evolutionarily wired, it is not in her power to extinguish her emotions. And even if it were, she would not want to extinguish them. They make it possible for her to take delight in small things, to feel joy and hope, and to love; indeed, they make it possible for her not simply to live but to flourish. A Thinker's goal, then, won't be to extinguish her emotions; it will be to keep them within proper bounds and, in particular, to prevent her head from being hijacked by her heart and gut. During her journey through life, she will, metaphorically speaking, keep her head in the driver's seat while restricting her heart and gut to the back seat. Although she can hear their comments and will sometimes accede to their requests, it will, to the extent possible, be *her* hands on the steering wheel.

A second misconception is that Thinkers will be intellectually imposing figures, and that becoming one requires an extensive education. Make these assumptions and you might worry that you aren't cut out to be a Thinker. Don't be discouraged, though. Consider fifth-century BCE philosopher Socrates. His education would have been rudimentary, and as a result he likely had a poorer understanding of his world and how it works than a modern sixth-grade student does.[3] It is nevertheless clear that Socrates habitually reasoned his way to conclusions. We might debate whether he was the *first* Thinker—probably not—but that he *was* a Thinker is indisputable. Furthermore, someone can fail to be a Thinker despite having an extensive education. This would be the case if the university he attended didn't foster students' critical thinking skills and didn't encourage open-mindedness—or even worse if his university, rather than teaching students *how* to think, told them *what* to think. It is also possible that although his university encouraged open-minded critical thinking, its efforts were wasted on him, for the simple reason that he doesn't like to think.

One other misconception is that Thinkers will be unanimous in their assessment of the truth of a claim. On the contrary, they not only can, but often will, disagree. This might be because one Thinker has access to evidence or information that another lacks, because two Thinkers have a different perspective on the same piece of evidence, or because one Thinker makes a logical or psychological error that another avoids. *As long as both individuals consciously engage in evidence-based, systematic thinking to arrive at their conclusions, both will count as Thinkers*, in the sense that I am using the term.

Of course, if two Thinkers disagree, they can't both be right, meaning that one of them is mistaken—or maybe that both are! Thinkers, in other words, are fallible. It is an unavoidable consequence of the semi-rational nature of human beings. On hearing this, some readers will be surprised and ask the obvious question: If becoming a Thinker doesn't guarantee attainment of the truth, then why become one? Because by thinking critically but with an open mind, we maximize our chance of filling that mind, to the extent possible, with true beliefs and thereby staying grounded in reality; indeed, it is because people have engaged in open-minded critical thinking that we know as much about the world as we do.

A Thinker will not only acknowledge that other Thinkers can disagree with her but will assume as much; indeed, she will seek out these contrary Thinkers. Although she might try to persuade them that they are making a mistake, she is open to the possibility that it is *she* who is mistaken—this is part of what is involved in being open-minded—and will therefore be curious about how they reached their conclusions. She also realizes that she and a contrary Thinker can *both* be mistaken. It could be, for example, that although they each have important insights into a subject, neither has a complete understanding of it. In such cases, both are likely to come away from their encounter with a better understanding of their world. These comments should make it clear that rather than coming across as intellectually imposing figures, Thinkers will be notable for their intellectual humility.

In conclusion, becoming a Thinker won't require you to extinguish your emotions or get an advanced degree. Nor will it require you to spend your days lost in profound thought. It will, however, require you to think more and in a different manner than you currently do. Anyone reading these words likely has the intellectual wherewithal to become a Thinker. If you are up to the challenge of doing so, read on.

A Look Ahead

In Part I of this book, we take a closer look at the act of believing, which turns out to be rather more complex than one might imagine. It is possible, for example, to be highly confident of a belief without being clear about what, exactly, you believe. You can also be convinced of the truth of a belief that is in fact mistaken, which can have disastrous consequences if you subsequently act on your misplaced convictions. Not only that, but you can—and in fact likely do—hold inconsistent beliefs. In Chapter 4, we explore this curious phenomenon.

In Part II, we examine the challenges that arise in sharing our beliefs. Words are ambiguous, and as a result even a simple sentence like "Cats sit" can have multiple meanings—fifty-six of them, to be exact. Often in conversation, people inadvertently use the same word in two different ways and as a result talk past each other. Such conversations can be deeply frustrating. Language can also cause us to tumble down the linguistic rabbit holes that philosopher Daniel Dennett refers to as *deepities*. Is love just a word? As we shall see, it depends.

To understand the world so we can predict and possibly affect the future, we need to understand causation, but causal chains are remarkably complex. In Part III, we examine their complexity and the manner in which a Thinker will respond to it. She will, to begin with, take a systematic approach to problem-solving, one that maximizes her chances of coming up with a solution that, although imperfect, is optimal, given her circumstances. She will also take a systematic approach to decision-making. She knows that because we live in a complex world, we should judge our decisions not by their consequences but by the process used to make them. A Thinker also knows that because she has to make so many decisions in daily life, it is reasonable to take mental shortcuts, some of which we will explore.

Because of our evolutionary past, we humans harbor cognitive biases that can derail our attempts to reason our way to conclusions. In Part IV, we explore these biases, paying particular attention to confirmation bias—our tendency to look for evidence that our beliefs are correct and avoid, ignore, or explain away evidence to the contrary—and to the Dunning–Kruger effect, which leads us to think we know more about a subject than we do. We also take a look at know-it-alls, at stupid people, and at people who, although not stupid, are willfully ignorant, in the sense that they go out of their way to avoid learning more about an event or phenomenon.

We end Part IV with an examination of the impact that the internet—and in particular, social media—has had on our thinking. The internet brought us search engines that made it easier to access information, but before long, those engines were reengineered in the name of profit. Instead of simply providing us with information relevant to our search, they told us things that, because they reinforced our current beliefs, we wanted to hear. This in turn increased the chance that we would come back and do more searches—and be exposed to more internet ads. Search engines were thereby transformed into confirmation-bias engines. The internet also provided platforms to people who previously would have been dismissed as crackpots, and they used these platforms to spew disinformation, conspiracy theories, and hate speech. In the process of doing so, they polluted the information space, thereby making it harder for people to stay grounded in reality. This alone would be bad, but social media made it possible for these individuals to find each other and form virtual tribes that disparaged the views of rival tribes. Discourse between the various tribes was fractious, and compromise between them became unthinkable, which is unfortunate because civil discourse and compromise are the lifeblood of democracy. And as if these problems weren't bad enough, the arrival of artificial intelligence will doubtless exacerbate them.

In Part V, I describe a Thinker's mind-optimization program, the first component of which is her *mindcare regimen*, the steps she takes to prevent mistaken beliefs from taking root in her mind. She will, in particular, be discriminating in her selection of sources of news and information, and will be circumspect in her use of search engines. Despite these mindcare efforts, mistaken beliefs will sometimes slip past her critical guard. Her mind-optimization program therefore has a second component: She will periodically engage in what I refer to as *mindcleaning*—not to be confused with brainwashing!—to find and eradicate those mistaken beliefs. Part of the mindcleaning process involves *stress-testing* her beliefs by finding and listening carefully to fellow Thinkers who reject them. These first two components of a Thinker's mind-optimization program—mindcare and mindcleaning—will tend to slow the growth of her belief set or even to shrink it. To stay grounded in an ever-changing reality, though, a Thinker will want to acquire new beliefs, and to achieve this goal, her mind-optimization program will include a third regimen, which I shall refer to as *mind expansion*: She will make a conscious effort to explore the world around her in search of beliefs that are both true and useful.

After describing a Thinker's mental regimens, I present a portrait of an archetypal Thinker. She is humble, inquisitive, skeptical, independent-minded, and open to criticism. She is also comfortable with uncertainty and complexity. In the final chapter of this book, I present readers with an "invitation to think," in the form of thought exercises. By doing them, readers will come to appreciate the satisfaction to be derived from thinking rather than feeling their way to a conclusion, as well as the impact that open-minded critical thinking can have on their life.

With some effort and guidance, you can learn how to think more and better—and maybe even transform yourself into a full-fledged Thinker. If you are up for this challenge, you've come to the right place!

PART I

Belief, Reconsidered

1 | What Does It Mean to Believe?

I believe many things, including that I have ten toes, two kidneys, and one gallbladder. I believe not only that George Washington was the first president of the United States but that he was a good president. I also believe that the universe began in a "Big Bang" and that Earth isn't the only place intelligent life exists.[1]

Besides having beliefs about things and events, I have beliefs about my beliefs. In particular, I believe that many of them are mistaken. If I knew which beliefs they were, trust me, I would abandon them. The problem is that false beliefs are skilled imposters. Believing something that is false will, to the person who believes it, feel the same as believing something that is true. We therefore can't distinguish our true beliefs from our false beliefs through introspection. We must instead do research, which will require time and effort on our part.

Because people are often reluctant to expend this time and effort, they end up holding false beliefs. You might, for example, believe that Napoleon Bonaparte was short, that humans evolved from monkeys, or that duck quacks don't echo. Although these beliefs are mistaken,[2] holding them is unlikely to harm the believer, but this is not always the case. An inebriated person's belief that he is still capable of driving a car can have deadly consequences, both for himself and for others.

Beliefs Can Be Empty or Fuzzy

Besides having a capacity for holding false beliefs, people have a capacity for holding beliefs that might be described as *empty*. In my philosophy classes, for example, our discussions periodically turned to religion. When I asked whether students believed in God, lots of hands would typically go up. I would then start a conversation about God. More precisely, I would ask the believers to fill me in: Who or what is God? Where is he? What does he do? These are questions that students typically struggled to answer.

One of the believers might inform me that God lives in heaven. My response: "Okay, but what and where is heaven, and what form does God take in his existence there? Does he have a physical body, and if so, is it a male or female body?" At this point, another believer might explain that God doesn't have a material body the way we do—that he is instead a "spirit being." My response: "Fine, but what's a 'spirit being'? All my life I've been hearing about them, but what, exactly, are they?" This confession of ignorance often surprised my students—surely I knew what a spirit being is!—and one of them might therefore offer what he took to be a helpful nudge: "You know, it's a being that exists simply as a spirit. No body or anything, just a spirit." But to no avail; I remained perplexed. This response, I should add, was quite sincere; indeed, to this day, I am puzzled by the concept of a spirit being.

At this point in the conversation, I would inform my students that although I was convinced that their belief in the existence of God was both deep and sincere, the belief in question seemed empty: *In believing in God, they didn't seem to know what they were believing.* I would go on to explain that it *is* possible to develop a non-empty belief in the existence of God; indeed, many theologians have done just that.[3] It would, however, require thought and effort on the part of students to "fill in" their belief—which presumably is exactly what God (assuming that he exists) would want them to do.

To be meaningful, a belief must have content. When you have an empty belief, it feels like you believe something, but you in fact believe nothing—nothing, at any rate, that you are able to give a coherent account of. Consequently, it is inaccurate to describe empty beliefs as being wrong. They are instead *worse than wrong* because they don't even rise to the level of being sufficiently coherent to be capable of being wrong.

If you want to discover which of your beliefs are empty, try to explain them to someone else—particularly to someone who doesn't share those beliefs and who, if she doesn't understand what you are saying, will ask for clarification. If a belief has content, such clarification will likely be easy,[4] but if it is empty, you will soon find yourself flummoxed. When a Thinker finds herself unable to explain what it is that she believes, she will respond by putting that belief "on hold" until such time as she can reconsider it and maybe infuse it with content.

Sometimes a belief is more appropriately described as being *fuzzy* rather than *empty*. The belief in question will clearly have *some* content; the problem is that the believer is unable to specify that content in any detail. I have had students, for example, who identify as socialists. When asked what socialism is, they might reply that socialists are in favor of universal healthcare. My response: "This isn't what socialism is; it is instead a proposal made by many of those who favor the core principles of socialism." If I went on to ask what those principles were, they struggled to answer. Students who instead identified as capitalists were often similarly fuzzy in their thinking.

Fuzzy beliefs are seductive in large part because of their "malleability." If you encounter evidence that a fuzzy belief is mistaken, you can respond by "adjusting" the belief to account for that evidence. Do this enough, and you will become confident that the belief is true, even though it is inchoate. Realize that this can be done unwittingly.

For Your Consideration: Answer the following questions. In doing so, resist the temptation to do an online search to increase your chances of answering correctly.

- Do you believe that London is the capital of England?
- Do you believe that Los Angeles is the capital of France?
- Do you believe that Yaren is the capital of the Republic of Nauru?

The State of Nonbelief

Chances are that you believe that London is the capital of England and don't believe that Los Angeles is the capital of France, but consider the question about Yaren. If you are like most readers, you are clueless with respect to Yaren and Nauru; indeed, you weren't even aware of their existence until you read the above question—which is precisely why I included it. You can therefore be described as someone who neither believes that Yaren *is* the capital of Nauru nor believes that it *isn't* the capital.

As a matter of logic, you either believe a statement or you don't. Realize, though, that there are two ways in which you can *not* believe a statement. The first is to "actively" *believe it to be false*, the way you "actively" believe that the statement "Los Angeles is the capital of France" is false. In other words, you can *disbelieve* the statement.[5] The second way to not believe a statement is to *neither* believe it to be true *nor* believe it to be false. This is likely your situation with respect to the statement that "Yaren is the capital of the Republic of Nauru." You don't believe it, but you don't disbelieve it, either. You instead have no beliefs regarding it.

It would be nice to have a word with which to describe this state of affairs. Allow me, therefore, to propose such a word: "nonbelieve."[6] A Thinker will want to include this word in her vocabulary. There will, after all, be lots of statements that she neither believes nor disbelieves. She knows that in the absence of convincing grounds for believing or disbelieving a statement, the rational thing to do is withhold judgment with respect to it; that is, to nonbelieve the statement—until such grounds become apparent, at which point she will be happy to exchange her nonbelief for either belief or disbelief.

Some people have an aversion to admitting that they don't have an opinion about a topic. They think that having lots of opinions—ideally, having an opinion about practically everything—will be taken as evidence of how smart they are. Ask them whether Yaren is the capital of the Republic of Nauru, and they might respond by forming a belief on the spot, presumably by hazarding a guess. A Thinker, by way of contrast, will freely admit to not having formed an opinion on a variety of topics, and if someone takes this as evidence of shallowness on her part, she will conclude that her critic isn't a particularly thoughtful person, meaning that his criticisms can be ignored. She knows that people who pride themselves on having opinions about nearly every topic are likely to have *considered* opinions about few topics. It is, however, these last opinions that a Thinker will value because the person who holds them will be able to give reasons for doing so—reasons that might persuade the Thinker to adopt them.

For Your Consideration: Tell whether you *believe*, *disbelieve*, or *nonbelieve* the following claims. Once again, resist the temptation to do an online search before you answer; instead, classify a claim in accordance with *your current state of belief.*

- $3 \times 2 = 6$.
- St. Paul is the capital of Minnesota.
- Bigfoot exists.
- Some bachelors are married.
- The people who claim to be your biological parents are *in fact* your biological parents.
- The author of this book is right-handed.
- There is currently a left mitten at the summit of Mount Everest.
- The death penalty ought to be abolished.

It turns out that there are two kinds of nonbelief. Consider the claim that there is currently a left mitten at the summit of Mount Everest—not that there *could be* a mitten there, but that there *actually is* one. It is likely that you have never given this claim a moment's thought, and under these circumstances, the reasonable thing for you to do is nonbelieve it. Let us refer to this as *naïve* nonbelief. Now consider the claim that the death penalty should be abolished. Suppose that although you have thought about this topic for many years, discussed it with many people, and read many articles about it, you still haven't made up your mind one way or the other. Under these circumstances, you will nonbelieve the claim, and the nonbelief in question can be characterized as *deliberate* because it is the result of careful thought.

To better appreciate the distinction between naïve and deliberate nonbelief, think about people's views regarding God's existence. We call someone who believes that God exists a *theist*,[7] someone who believes that God doesn't exist an *atheist*, and someone who nonbelieves that God exists an *agnostic*. This means that there are two different kinds of agnostics. There are, to begin with, people who nonbelieve that God exists for the simple reason that they have never given the matter any thought—perhaps because they have never heard of him, the way you (likely) had never heard of Yaren. Let us refer to these individuals as *naïve agnostics*. There are also people who have not only heard of God but have thought long and hard about whether he exists, only to conclude that they don't yet have sufficient evidence to make up their mind. Let us refer to them as *deliberate agnostics*.

A Question of Confidence

Consider again the exercise in which I asked whether you believed, disbelieved, or nonbelieved a list of claims. Although you likely believed that $3 \times 2 = 6$, that the people who claim to be your biological parents are in fact your biological parents, and that the author of this book is right-handed, your confidence in the truth of these claims probably varied. Whereas you felt certain that $3 \times 2 = 6$, you were—assuming that you are a thoughtful person—a little less than certain that the people who claim to be your biological parents are in fact your biological parents. (It could be, after all, that you are adopted and that your adoptive parents are keeping it a secret. It could also be that although the people you take to be your biological parents sincerely believe that they *are* your biological parents, there was an unfortunate mix-up at the hospital at which you were born. Such things happen!) And finally, if you believe that the author of this book is right-handed, you should at most be "rather confident" that your belief is correct. This belief, after all, is likely based on the generalization that *the vast majority of people* are right-handed, but maybe I am among those who aren't.

A Thinker will be more confident of the truth of some claims than others and will be mindful of her differing levels of confidence. Furthermore, only in special cases will she allow herself the luxury of feeling certain that a claim is true. She will likewise be reluctant to feel certain that a claim is false. Ask whether she feels certain that the claim that some bachelors are married is false, and she will answer that she does, since by definition, bachelors are unmarried. Ask whether she is likewise certain that the claim that Bigfoot exists is false, and she might reply that although she is highly confident that Bigfoot doesn't exist, since so many searches for him have come up empty-handed, she is not *certain* that he doesn't exist. There is, after all, a slim chance that he does.

Another thing to realize about the above claims is that different people will have different levels of conviction with respect to the truth of a claim. For example, residents of Minnesota—and in particular, residents of St. Paul—will likely be highly confident of their belief about whether St. Paul is the capital of Minnesota, but residents of, say, Nevada will likely have a harder time deciding what to believe, and residents of the Republic of Nauru might tell us that they have no idea whatsoever whether St. Paul is the capital of Minnesota, the way you are probably in the dark about whether Yaren is the capital of the Republic of Nauru. They will, in other words, nonbelieve the claim that St. Paul is the capital of Minnesota.

It is tempting to think of belief as being binary, the way an old-fashioned light switch is. In the same way as those switches are either on or off, you either believe something or you don't. The foregoing discussion reveals, however, that belief is more like a modern dimmer switch. More precisely, belief admits of degree: You are more confident of some beliefs than others. Or shifting the simile, belief is like the wind. In the same way as wind has both a direction and a velocity, your beliefs have both content and a level of confidence. A Thinker's level of confidence with respect to a belief will depend on the quantity and quality of the available evidence. Ask whether she believes that St. Paul is the capital of Minnesota, and she might respond, "Yes, I do. More precisely, I am somewhat confident that it is. I guess a part of me thinks that Minneapolis *should be* the capital, but I will go with St. Paul."

We have seen that false beliefs are imposters. From the perspective of the believer, holding a false belief feels exactly the same as holding a true belief. Beliefs we are certain about, however, feel quite different than beliefs about which we are only highly confident. In the latter case, we leave open the possibility that a belief is mistaken, and we might worry about this. By feeling certain that a belief is true, we eliminate those anxieties. Furthermore, if someone challenges a belief that we feel certain is true, we can comfortably dismiss the challenge without thinking twice—from our point of view, the challenger is surely mistaken.

Because certainty feels good, people crave it. They can simply fake the feeling, but with a little effort, they can induce it within themselves by doing a bit of guided—or should I say misguided?—research. More precisely, they can seek out sources that support their beliefs and carefully avoid sources that challenge them. The good feelings that accompany this certainty, however, are like the good feelings that accompany the use of heroin: Although it initially feels good, it can later reduce the user to a state of misery. If you feel certain that a belief is true, you will be more willing to act on it; and if it subsequently turns out to be false, your actions can have disastrous consequences. It's unfortunate if you get hurt, but then again, you will be paying the price for your own stupidity. What is tragic is when *other people* end up paying a price for your stupidity.

For the record, St. Paul is indeed the capital of Minnesota, and the author of this book is right-handed. Furthermore, Yaren is *not* the capital city of the Republic of Nauru, but not for the reason you might expect. It isn't because some other city is its capital but because Nauru has no official capital city. Furthermore, Yaren is a district, not a city.

Beliefs Can Be Black and White, Hot and Cold

Some people have what might be called a *black-and-white belief system*. When presented with a statement, they will tend either to believe that it is true or to believe that it is false, and they will be confident that their belief is correct. A Thinker, by way of contrast, will consciously harbor many nonbeliefs, and when she does believe or disbelieve a statement, her level of confidence will be proportional to the quantity and quality of the evidence available to her. We might therefore describe her as believing *in shades of gray.*

More generally, a Thinker will resist binary labels. If asked whether personality is the result of nature or nurture, she might answer that both play a role. If asked whether she is pro-life or pro-choice, she might answer that she is neither and go on to describe cases in which she is confident that abortion would be morally permissible, cases in which she is confident that it would be morally impermissible, and cases about which she has yet to make up her mind. Her thinking with respect to abortion, in other words, will be nuanced. And if asked whether she is politically liberal or conservative, a Thinker might answer that she is *both* liberal *and* conservative, and go on to explain that she is, say, staunchly conservative with respect to economic issues but liberal-leaning with respect to social issues.

People can be emotionally attached to a belief, making it for them what might be called a *hot belief.* You can take the temperature of your beliefs by watching how you respond when someone challenges them. Suppose, for example, that when someone challenges your belief about the morality of abortion, you feel your blood pressure rise. As a result, you might find yourself yelling at the challenger. This is compelling evidence that, for you, the belief in question is red hot.

Now suppose someone challenges your belief that $5 + 2 = 7$. You would likely be puzzled that he would do such a thing and might try to straighten him out with a little demonstration: "Look, I am holding up five fingers. Now I will hold up two more. Let's count how many fingers I am holding up. See, there are seven fingers up! So, five plus two equals seven."[8] If this demonstration didn't convince him, you probably wouldn't get angry at him—at least I hope you wouldn't because that would be a pointless waste of time and energy. You would instead take pity on him, and after politely excusing yourself, you would calmly go about your business. Conclusion: Although you are supremely confident that 5 + 2 = 7, the belief is, for you, ice cold.

Your cold beliefs typically originate in your head, which takes the evidence available to you and dispassionately draws conclusions about what to believe. If someone challenges these beliefs, your head can simply recount the process by which it reached them, meaning that there is no reason for you to get angry. Your hot beliefs, by way of contrast, originate in your heart or gut, meaning that a justification for believing them won't be ready at hand. On realizing as much, you might become upset or even angry at getting challenged. In the words of philosopher Bertrand Russell, "If an opinion contrary to your own makes you angry, that is a sign that you are subconsciously aware of having no good reason for thinking as you do."[9]

Belief, then, is more complicated than one might imagine. For one thing, it isn't the case that you either believe something or you don't, and when you do believe something, the intensity of your belief can—and should!—vary. Furthermore, you can believe something without being clear about what, exactly, it is that you believe. You can also become enthralled by a belief.

So how, exactly, do we come to hold the beliefs that we do? It is to this question that we now turn our attention.

2 | Coming to Believe

There was a time when you didn't believe that Brazil is in South America; indeed, there was a time when you didn't even believe that Brazil and South America existed. There was also a time when you didn't believe that you had a gallbladder and didn't believe that the book you are currently reading existed. You now believe these things. How did this happen? More generally, what are the ways in which you come to believe something?

Many of your beliefs are the result of direct experience. You might believe that you are hungry because you feel hunger pangs, and you might believe that there is a cell phone in your hand because you can see and feel it there. Such beliefs can be mistaken, though. To a man in the desert, it might look like there is a pool of water off in the distance, but when he walks to it, it vanishes. It was just a mirage. It isn't necessary to go to a desert to experience an illusion, though. Take certain drugs, and you will hallucinate. If you are averse to using drugs, you can instead take a nap. With some luck, you will dream during it, and in your dreams you will see, hear, and touch imaginary things.

Other beliefs can be traced back to physical evidence. Detectives, for example, might come to believe that someone committed a murder on the basis of the fingerprints and blood spatters found at the crime scene. Physical evidence can also take the form of pictures and videos. Suppose, for example, that the detectives obtain a photo of their suspect entering the home where the murder took place. Before relying on it, they should consider the possibility that the photo, although genuine, was taken long before the murder. And if the photo was not only taken just before the murder but shows the man holding a gun, they should consider the possibility that the photo was altered. This is why, if our goal is mind optimization, it is important for us to become reflexively skeptical.

If direct experience is the basis for our beliefs about the present, memories are often the basis for our beliefs about the past. We believe that we ate breakfast, for example, because we remember doing so. It turns out, though, that our memory can be as deceptive as our senses. For one thing, it is possible to plant in someone's mind the memory of an event that never took place. Furthermore, with the passage of time your memories can change of their own accord. Your mental image of your childhood home might be shattered by seeing a picture your parents took of that house. Along similar lines, someone might interrupt the autobiographical story you are telling to inform you that this isn't the first time you've told the tale and that the previous time you told it, the details were different. Memories, in other words, are malleable, meaning that memory-based beliefs can be mistaken.

Furthermore, research indicates that eyewitness testimony, in which a person sincerely reports what he remembers seeing, isn't necessarily trustworthy.[1] Many people fail to realize this, though, and as a result, challenging their testimony is, from their point of view, tantamount to accusing them of lying. This, however, is an overreaction. In challenging them, you are not questioning their sincerity; you are simply questioning the reliability of their senses and memory.

Inferred Beliefs

Pay attention to your belief-formation process, and you will discover that many of your new beliefs are the result of inferences drawn from beliefs you already hold. Suppose, for example, that you hear a rushing noise outside your window and thereby come to believe that it is raining. Although the belief that you hear a noise is acquired through direct experience, the belief that rain is its source is inferred. Now suppose that a few minutes after hearing the rushing noise, a flash of light illuminates the room in which you are sitting. You might now infer two new beliefs: that what was going on wasn't simply a rainstorm but a thunderstorm, and that in a few seconds, you will hear thunder.

For a more subtle example of an inferential belief, consider the following question: Do you have more toes on your left foot than a zebra has legs? It is unlikely that you have ever given this question a moment's thought and therefore have no beliefs whatsoever regarding it. Given a moment, though, you can infer its answer from three beliefs you do possess: That you have five toes on your left foot, that zebras have four legs, and that five is more than four. Your conclusion: Yes, you do believe that you have more toes on your left foot than a zebra has legs.

If I go on to ask whether you believe that zebras wear striped pajamas, you will likewise be able to form a belief by inference, even though you have never given the matter a moment's thought. Because you believe that zebras don't wear clothes, you infer that they don't wear pajamas in general and don't wear striped pajamas in particular. Had you lacked beliefs about zebras' clothes-wearing propensities, or even worse, if you had lacked beliefs about zebras because you were unaware of their existence, your answer to my question would be "I don't know."

These are conscious inferences, but for each such inference, there will be many more that are unconscious. As you go about your daily business, for example, you continually form beliefs about your environment and about how your actions will affect your sensory perceptions. Psychologists refer to this belief-formation phenomenon as *predictive processing*.[2] Normally you will be oblivious to these beliefs and will become aware of their existence only if your subsequent experience disproves them. Suppose, for example, that you are taking an elevator on a visit to the dentist. You reach the floor you requested, but when the doors open, you see a sandy beach as well as waves breaking on the nearby shoreline. You will be not merely startled but stunned. Had you not unconsciously formed a belief about how things would appear when the elevator doors opened, though, you would not have had this reaction.

For Your Consideration: Take a moment to determine whether or not you believe the following equations to be true. Pay attention to the process you use to make your determination. Do not use a calculator!

- $3 \times 2 = 6$.
- $4{,}583 \times 972 = 7{,}246$.
- $4{,}583 \times 972 = 4{,}454{,}674$.
- $19 \times 17 = 323$.

In considering the above equations, you likely believed that $3 \times 2 = 6$ because you had memorized this math fact back in grade school. It is unlikely that you had ever considered the product of 4,583 and 972, but on the basis of your beliefs about how multiplication works, you might have inferred that the product *couldn't* be 7,246 because that number simply isn't big enough. Likewise, you might have inferred that the product of 4,583 and 972 *couldn't* be 4,454,674. This product looks big enough, but because the rightmost digits of 4,583 and 972 are 3 and 2, respectively, the rightmost digit of their product will be $3 \times 2 = 6$ rather than 4, so their product *couldn't* be 4,454,674. With respect to the equation $19 \times 17 = 323$, though, shortcut inferences like these aren't possible. The product given looks big enough and has the right last digit— namely a 3 because $9 \times 7 = 63$—but is that product correct? To find out, you not only have to engage in inferential thinking, but the inferences are complicated enough to require several seconds to complete.

Our inferential ability allows us to bring new beliefs into existence as needed. Almost everyone can remember the multiplication tables up to 10×10. Few people are capable of memorizing them up to 100×100, though. It is therefore wonderful that a basic understanding of the multiplication process allows us to form innumerably many new beliefs about the result of multiplying two numbers. Give me a pencil and paper, and in a minute or two I will tell you the product of 4,583 and 972. In other, more complicated cases, it might take hours or even days to tell you what I (inferentially) believe.

So how big is our belief set? We have very many conscious beliefs. Add to them the beliefs we can infer from those beliefs, as well as the unconscious beliefs we hold as the result of predictive processing, and the resulting set will be truly enormous.

Believing What We Are Told

Trace the history of your beliefs and you will find that many of them weren't formed as the result of direct experience, physical evidence, or even by drawing inferences from previously held beliefs. They can instead be traced back to what someone told you. You inherit many things from your parents, including, most significantly, your genes. You might also inherit, in some weaker sense of the word, your personality, as well as physical objects, like the tea set they inherited from *their* parents. Your parents are also the source of many of your beliefs, though, including most of your basic beliefs about how the world works, such as your belief that carrots are edible, that snow is frozen water, and that germs cause illness. Many children also "inherit" their parents' religious and political beliefs. Realize, though, that in much the same way as your genes would be different if you had been born to different parents, many of your beliefs would also be different if you had been raised by different parents. A significant portion of your belief set is therefore an accident of birth—or in some cases, adoption.

As you age, you acquire additional beliefs from your siblings, cousins, aunts, uncles, and grandparents. Your friends are another source of beliefs. Many things my childhood friends told me turned out to be mistaken—such as that the foods I eat go to different parts of my body, with meat going to my thighs and carrots going to my fingers. Because my youthful self had an extremely open mind and limited critical thinking ability, I was a belief sponge and, more often than not, believed what they told me. After all, their claims made perfect sense.

When you started school, you probably didn't challenge the truth of what you were taught. You simply assumed that if something was false, your teachers wouldn't go to the trouble of teaching it. In high school, greater emphasis was placed on developing your critical thinking skills. Besides being told what to believe, you might have been shown why it should be believed. In geometry class, for example, you were asked to prove various propositions, and in chemistry class, you did experiments to test predictions made on the basis of chemical theory. A college education can play an important role in helping transform students into Thinkers, but in many colleges, critical-thinking courses aren't required, and when they are, they might be spent teaching, say, syllogistic logic and avoidance of the classical fallacies rather than fostering open-minded critical thinking.

Even when open-mindedness is officially encouraged at their college, students might discover that some viewpoints are not open to discussion in some classes. As a result, it is entirely possible to graduate from college with both limited critical thinking ability and a mind that is only half open. I should add that many professors, particularly in the liberal arts, wouldn't regard this outcome as a failure, as long as what students came away believing was a close approximation of what their professors believed. The professors in question, after all, might be convinced that what they think is correct and that by telling their students what to think, they are saving them the trouble of having to discover the truth on their own. Not only that, but because many of their students lack critical thinking skills, professors worry that, if left to their own devices, these students would form erroneous beliefs. Really, they are doing their students a favor by telling them what to think! Of course, in assuming that their students aren't capable of thinking for themselves, these professors are acknowledging that their university has failed them in one important respect.

The Role of Surrogate Thinkers

As infants, we simply accept the truth of what we are told, but with the passing years we start deciding for ourselves whether or not to believe what people tell us. We also become aware of a curious phenomenon. If we don't like to exercise, we can't get someone else to exercise on our behalf. If we don't like to think, though, we *can* get someone else to think on our behalf; indeed, many people are happy to do so. Salespeople, for example, are quite willing to play the role of surrogate thinker. They will walk us through the ways to pay for a car or house and thereby demonstrate that we can indeed "afford" it. Advocacy journalists are willing to play this role with respect to current events. They will explain their significance and maybe even tell us whom to vote for in an upcoming election. Cult leaders are likewise happy to think on our behalf, and in this role, they will tell us what to do with our money and how to spend our days.

In choosing a surrogate thinker, we might pay particular attention to his level of confidence with respect to the claims he makes. Confidence, after all, is evidence of competence, right? And besides outsourcing our thinking to individuals, we might outsource it to crowds, on the assumption that whatever most people believe is probably true; otherwise, why would they believe it?

When considering a controversial topic, lots of people outsource their thinking to someone who has very strong opinions about very many subjects and is eager to defend the correctness of those opinions. These *argufiers*, as they are called,[3] regard conversations as debates to be won, preferably with an audience on hand to admire their victory. In these debates, they won't admit to being unsure of something or, even worse, to being ignorant of it. They will instead exude confidence in the truth of their claims because this is the best way to impress an audience. They might also obfuscate and quibble in an attempt to tip the odds of "victory" in their favor. And not to be forgotten, they might obsess over having the last word in an argument. They will take this as evidence of having won the argument, when in fact their interlocutor might simply have decided to abandon a pointless conversation.

By way of contrast, a Thinker will typically eschew debates in favor of thoughtful conversations. Furthermore, she will regard those conversations as collaborative encounters in which to explore her beliefs as well as those of her interlocutor. By having such conversations, she can potentially affect what someone else believes, but at the same time she can look for mistakes in her own belief set. And if her interlocutor is unable to respond to the points she raises, she will not gloat. She will instead take it as an opportunity to nudge him toward the truth—or maybe toward a reduced level of certainty with respect to his mistaken beliefs.

Some people, to make up their mind about a topic, watch a debate between contrary argufiers. When the debate is over, they outsource their thinking to whoever, in their opinion, won the debate: Whatever he thinks about the topic, that's what *they* think. Alternatively, they might adopt the views of whoever the audience thinks won the debate. People who have already made up their mind about a topic might also watch argufiers debate it, but there is a danger that instead of using the event as an opportunity to thoughtfully reconsider their views, they will simply side with whoever is advocating those views and will come away even more confident of them.

You might assume that an independent-minded Thinker would refuse to outsource her thinking, but this isn't the case. She is well aware that she doesn't know everything and will therefore periodically seek expert help. When tax time rolls around, for example, she might seek the help of a tax consultant, and if she notices an ominous swelling in her abdomen, she will seek the help of a physician.

That said, she will choose her experts with care. She might, in particular, look for evidence of expertise in the form of diplomas and certifications. And even though she is not an expert in an area, she will make a point of testing the credibility of potential surrogate thinkers by asking them to justify the advice they provide. If they are willing to answer her questions, and if their answers seem coherent and evidence-based, she will be reassured, but if they discourage or even forbid such questions, she will go elsewhere for help. She won't take confidence as evidence of competence and will therefore distrust "experts" who are certain that their advice is correct. A reliable expert, she knows, will be willing and able to lay out for her the ways in which the course of action he is recommending can go awry. What she will seek, in other words, is someone who engages in open-minded critical thinking with respect to a field.

When one of her beliefs is challenged, a Thinker will be able to defend it, but the form of the defense will vary. Challenge her belief that it is raining, and she might offer a mix of eyewitness testimony and physical evidence: "I just came in and look how soaked I am." Challenge her belief that the world is round,[4] though, and she might offer a more elaborate justification:

> I have seen pictures taken from space, and in those pictures the earth is round. During the lunar eclipses I have watched, the edge of the earth's shadow is curved rather than straight, which is not what you would expect if the earth were flat. I have also had phone calls and video conferences with people around the world, and although it was morning where I was, it might have been noon or the middle of the night where they were. If you look at where they were on a globe, you will see that unlike the "flat earth hypothesis," the "round earth hypothesis" does an excellent job of explaining why this should be so.

Challenge her rather more complex belief that protons are heavier than electrons, and unless she is a physicist, she is unlikely to have a justification at hand. She will instead resort to surrogate thinkers and, in particular, to scientists who arrived at this conclusion by means of careful thought, observation, and experimentation.

Besides outsourcing some of her thinking to carefully chosen experts, a Thinker will sometimes rely on "the wisdom of crowds." She might, for example, look at online ratings when buying a thermos, and she might try the new restaurant her friends are raving about. In these cases, after all, the stakes aren't very high, and by acting on other people's advice, she can determine whether or not to rely on their advice in the future.

In many other cases, though, she will distrust what "most people" think. She knows that it is entirely possible that *no one* in a crowd relied on evidence-based systematic thinking to reach their conclusion. She also knows that some of history's greatest tragedies were the result of the mistaken thinking of crowds. In Salem, Massachusetts, in the 1690s, for example, citizens were convinced that witches were at work in their village, and as a result twenty innocent people were executed.[5] Nineteen of them were hanged. The twentieth, a farmer named Giles Corey, was stripped naked and staked to the ground. A plank was placed on him, on top of which stones were slowly added until, three days later, he breathed his last.[6] Like I say, tragic. And realize that the groupthink phenomenon, besides afflicting villages, can afflict entire nations.

3 | Proving and Disproving Claims

People make claims all the time, but *proving* them can be difficult. To see why, consider the simple claim that your neighbor—let us call him John—is married. Suppose you went to the local courthouse but found no license there. That wouldn't prove that John isn't married: You might have overlooked his license, or maybe the license is at some other courthouse. Now suppose you did find a license there. Although it would count as evidence that he is married, it wouldn't conclusively prove as much. There is, after all, a chance that the license you saw was a fake planted by John, or that the license is real but John subsequently got a divorce. There is also a (very remote) chance that you only dreamed that you had gone to the courthouse and seen the license. The fact that such things can happen means that you can never prove *conclusively* that John is married. The best you can do is come up with evidence that will make a reasonable person highly confident, but by no means certain, that he is married. In what follows, this is what I will mean when I talk about "proving" claims.

Now consider the slightly more complex claim that John and his brother Sam are *both* married. Because of its logical structure, proving this claim will take more effort than proving that John is married. Proving it, after all, will require us to investigate the marital status of not one but two individuals. Suppose, however, that in our investigation of John's marital status, we come up with convincing evidence that he is *not* married. Even though we haven't begun our investigation of Sam, we will have disproved the conjunctive claim that John and Sam are *both* married. Lucky us.

In this chapter, we will examine what is involved in proving and disproving various kinds of claims. We will see that in some cases it is easier to prove a claim than to disprove it; that in other cases it is easier to disprove a claim than to prove it; and that in yet other cases, either proving or disproving a claim will require a fair amount of effort on our part. We will also discover that although proving or disproving most claims requires gathering evidence and doing research, some claims can be proved or disproved simply by telling stories—by performing what philosophers and scientists refer to as *thought experiments*. And finally, we will explore the "burden-of-proof" concept: When someone makes a claim that we don't agree with, is it his job to provide evidence that the claim is true or is it our job to disprove it?

Proving and Disproving Generalizations

Besides making specific claims about things and people, we generalize about them. In a *universal* generalization, we assert that *everything* in a certain group has a certain property. Whereas the claim that "Everyone has a gallbladder" generalizes about people, the claim that "All poodles are dogs" generalizes about poodles. Instead of generalizing about things, we can generalize about times—"Bob *always* loses his keys"—and generalize about places—"Bob has looked *everywhere* for his keys." We can also "negatively generalize." Saying that *no one* is over ten feet tall is logically equivalent to saying that *everyone* is *not* over ten feet tall.[1] Likewise, saying that Bob is *never* on time for meetings is just another way of saying that he is *always* late for them.

Proving a universal generalization will typically require considerable effort. To prove, for example, that everyone has a gallbladder, we will have to track down and inspect *every living person*—no small undertaking. Even though the first million people we inspect have a gallbladder, there will be billions left to inspect. Furthermore, in the unlikely event that we succeed in tracking down and inspecting every living person and find that they all have gallbladders, it is possible that the first person we inspected when we started our investigation subsequently had his removed, meaning that although every person we inspected had a gallbladder *at the time we individually inspected them*, not everyone *currently does*. We can avoid these difficulties by generalizing not about everyone or everything, but about everyone or everything in a restricted group. For example, for me to prove that every book on my office bookshelf is written in English will require minimal time and effort.

It is usually easier to disprove a universal generalization than to prove one. To see why this is so, suppose we set out to determine whether every living person has a gallbladder, and suppose that by sheer luck, the very first person we examine lacks one: It had been surgically removed to deal with painful gallstone attacks. We will thereby have disproved the claim that everyone has a gallbladder, and the individual *sans* gallbladder will constitute what logicians call a *counterexample*: He is a single instance that disproves a universal generalization. A Thinker will be adept at coming up with counterexamples. Indeed, utter a universal generalization in her presence, and you might notice a distracted look on her face as she tries to come up with a counterexample. Tell her that all birds can fly, and she might, after a few seconds, respond with a question: "What about penguins?"

Because she knows that universal generalizations are hard to prove, a Thinker will think twice before asserting one. She might feel comfortable asserting, say, that all triangles have three sides or that all bachelors are unmarried because these claims are true by definition. She might also be comfortable asserting that *nearly* everyone has a gallbladder. She will, however, be leery of making generalizations about *everyone*. She doesn't, after all, want to be on the receiving end of a counterexample.

Whereas *universal* generalizations make claims about *all* things, *statistical* generalizations make claims about *nearly all* things, *most* things, *many* things, *a few* things, or maybe *a specific percentage* of things.[2] The claim that nearly everyone has a gallbladder is therefore a statistical generalization, as are the claims that most adults are over five feet tall, that 51 percent of people are female, and that few people are left-handed. Proving or disproving a statistical generalization will typically require a middling amount of effort on our part. Proving or disproving the claim that *few* people are left-handed, for example, will require us to survey perhaps a hundred randomly chosen people. Proving or disproving the more precise claim that *11 percent of people* are left-handed, however, will require us to survey a rather larger number of people. Although these surveys will require effort on our part, it will be much less than is required to prove, say, that everyone has a gallbladder.

We have seen that we can disprove a universal generalization by finding a single counterexample. This is not the case with statistical generalizations, though. You cannot, for example, disprove the claim that *nearly* everyone has a gallbladder by identifying a relative who had his removed. The claim, after all, is not that *everyone* has a gallbladder; it is that *nearly* everyone does, and "nearly everyone" allows for exceptions, such as your relative.

Claims of Necessity

When I assert that I have a gallbladder, I am making a claim about what is *in fact* the case. Suppose, however, I assert that I *necessarily* have a gallbladder. This is a rather stronger claim because it asserts not only that I have a gallbladder but that it is *inconceivable* that I would lack one. I *can* conceive of this situation, though; I can, in particular, imagine that a year ago, as the result of a gallstone attack, mine was surgically removed. No, this didn't happen, but because it *could have* happened, it isn't necessarily true that I have a gallbladder.

For examples of correct claims of necessity, we can turn to mathematics: The proposition that $1 + 1 = 2$ doesn't just happen to be true, it is necessarily true. We can also turn to logic: The disjunctive claim that I either have a gallbladder or don't have a gallbladder is necessarily true. And we can turn to semantics: The claim that every bachelor is unmarried is necessarily true. Being unmarried, after all, is part of what it means to be a bachelor.

We can't refute claims of fact by telling stories. We can't, in particular, refute the claim that everyone (in fact) has a gallbladder by telling a story about a person who lacks one. We must instead go out and find such a person. We can, however, refute claims of necessity by telling stories. This is what I did when I raised the possibility of having had my gallbladder removed last year. Realize, though, that the story we tell must be internally consistent; otherwise, the story wouldn't describe a conceivable state of affairs. Suppose, for example, that we try to refute the claim that triangles are necessarily three-sided by telling a story about a two-sided triangle. Such an entity is inconceivable, meaning that this story won't do the job. The same would be the case if we tried to refute the claim that bachelors are necessarily unmarried by telling a story about a married bachelor.

Claims of necessity are, at base, a special kind of universal generalization: Instead of generalizing about people, things, or times, they generalize about conceivable states of affairs. More precisely, they claim that something is true under *every* conceivable state of affairs. We can therefore provide a counterexample to such claims by telling an internally consistent story that describes a possible state of affairs in which they would be false. A Thinker will therefore be very careful about making claims of necessity. She knows how strong they are and doesn't want to be on the receiving end of such a story.

Proving and Disproving Existential Claims

Besides making specific claims or generalizing about the properties of existing things, we can make what are called *existential claims*, in which we assert that certain things or things of a certain type exist. The assertion that Bigfoot exists is an existential claim, as is the claim that some elephants weigh more than seven tons. (And in case you are wondering, what I am referring to as "existential claims" have nothing to do with the core claims made by the philosophers known as existentialists.)

We have seen that it is typically harder to prove a universal generalization than to disprove one, but the opposite is often the case with respect to existential claims. To prove that Bigfoot exists—more precisely, that a Bigfoot-type creature exists—we would have to track one down and capture it, something that apparently is difficult to do. Proving that such a creature *doesn't* exist, however, would be harder still. We would have to scour the world trying to find him but fail to do so. Likewise, to prove that *some elephants weigh more than seven tons*, I need to find only one. To disprove this claim, though, I will have to track down and weigh elephants around the globe and not find a single seven-tonner, a weighty undertaking.

Let us pause to examine the claim one sometimes hears, that you can't prove a negative. It is a strange claim to make because the claim itself is a negative—it is a claim about what you *can't* do—meaning that it is a claim that the person making it can't prove! Setting this problem aside, let's assume that what he is trying to say is that you can't prove that something doesn't exist. This indeed is sometimes the case. Consider, for example, a sphere of pure gold that is precisely 10,000 meters in diameter. Proving that such an object doesn't exist would involve a search of the entire universe—an impossible undertaking. In other cases, however, we *can* prove that something doesn't exist. To prove the nonexistence of a seven-ton elephant perched atop the Eiffel Tower, for example, we need only go there and not find one. Thus, the claim that you can't prove a negative is questionable, to say the least.

From the mere fact that we lack evidence that something *does* exist, it does not follow that it *doesn't* exist. Indeed, even if we make a concerted effort to find something and come up empty-handed, it doesn't follow that the thing in question doesn't exist. A Thinker will realize as much, and if you ask her whether Bigfoot exists, she might respond that given the numerous failed attempts to find him and the low quality of the evidence that has been produced—including, most famously, grainy sixteen-millimeter film footage dating back to 1967[3]—she thinks his existence is highly unlikely. But because she is open-minded, she won't rule out the possibility that he does indeed exist. Her mind, in other words, will be open with respect to the existence of Bigfoot, but open just a crack.

Scientists, by the way, aren't necessarily open-minded. Some won't even entertain the idea that Bigfoot exists. They might fear that doing this will not only give credence to speculation about Bigfoot but might undermine their reputation as serious scientists. Geneticist Brian Sykes is one notable exception to this propensity. He and his colleagues put out a call to the "Bigfoot community" for hair samples thought to have come from "anomalous primates," including Bigfoot and the Yeti. They received fifty-seven samples from around the world and set about examining them. Some turned out to be plant fibers rather than hair, and others were too old or damaged to be usable. They did genetic analyses of the rest, but all came from known animals. They found cow hair, bear hair, porcupine hair, and even human hair, but none that could be attributed to an anomalous primate.[4]

Proving and Disproving Theories

Because we live in an orderly universe, the future is predictable—not perfectly predictable, but somewhat so. This means that our ancestors who looked for regularities in nature and assumed that they would continue into the future were more likely to survive than those who didn't. As their brainpower increased, so did their ability to detect regularities and make predictions on the basis of them. At one time, our ancestors would simply have believed that *When dropped, objects fall.* This hypothesis would later have been refined—*When dropped, objects fall straight down*—and subsequently it would have been refined even further—*When dropped, objects fall straight down, and the longer they fall, the faster they fall.*[5] Some of our ancestors also concluded that heavy objects fall faster than light objects, but Galileo did his famous experiment and discovered otherwise. Because of his use of what we now think of as the scientific method, Galileo is a leading contender for the title of "father of modern science."

Besides making predictions about *what* will happen under certain circumstances, scientists develop theories to explain *why* things happen the way they do. The theory of gravity, for example, posits that the mass of an object gives rise to a gravitational field that will attract any other object with mass. These fields can't be seen, but their presence can be demonstrated, perhaps by dropping a ball. Such theories give us insight into why the world works as it does. After very many observations under a wide variety of circumstances, scientists might become so confident of the correctness of a theory that they start referring to it as a *law*. We need to keep in mind, however, that scientific "laws" not only can be but have been overturned.[6]

Scientific theories vary dramatically in their content, but one thing they have in common is that they are falsifiable. Notice that I did not say that they are *false*; indeed, we have reason to think they are true. What I said is that they are *falsifiable*, in the sense that we can *imagine* them being disproved by new evidence. You might think it would be a good thing for a theory *not* to be falsifiable because this would mean that it could never be disproved, which in turn would mean that it has to be true—right? Although this line of reasoning is tempting, a Thinker will reject it. Indeed, she will have little patience for theories that are not falsifiable. This is because such theories are useless.

To see why I say this, consider the *theory of divine providence*, according to which, whatever happens is God's will. You won the lottery? It is because God wanted you to. You instead lost the lottery? It must have been God's will that you lose. You broke your arm cycling? Again, it was God's will. It soon becomes apparent that no matter what happens, the event in question will not count as evidence against the theory of divine providence; indeed, it can instead be taken as evidence in support of it! What more could anyone want of a theory?

In response to this question, a Thinker will point out that a theory capable of explaining whatever happens in the future is useless for predicting future events. Someone who believes in the theory of gravity will be able to make quite precise predictions about what will happen if you drop a ball: It will fall straight down at an accelerating velocity. Someone who believes in divine providence, however, will be unable to predict any aspect of the future. He might predict that things will happen in accordance with God's will, but because we can't know God's will until God reveals it, this prediction will be of no value to us here and now. A Thinker will therefore dismiss unfalsifiable theories in favor of theories that, although falsifiable, are in fact true.

Astrology, by the way, is a falsifiable theory: It makes predictions that not only *can be* disproved but routinely *are*. Conclusion: Besides being *falsifiable*, astrology is *just plain false*.

Astrologers have responded to this lamentable state of affairs by filling their horoscopes with advice rather than predictions,[7] and when they do stick their necks out and predict, they keep their predictions vague or ambiguous, so their mistakes won't be obvious. The ancient Oracle of Delphi employed this same strategy. King Croesus asked her whether he should make war on the Persians. She replied that if he went to war against Cyrus the Great, a mighty empire would be destroyed. On hearing this advice, Croesus went to war, but instead of destroying Cyrus's empire, he destroyed his own.

The Burden of Proof

The "burden-of-proof" concept plays a role in many courts of law. In American jurisprudence, for example, a defendant does not have to prove his innocence to be exonerated; it is instead up to the prosecution to prove his guilt. A Thinker will routinely employ the burden-of-proof concept but in a somewhat different manner. In her discussions with other people, she will proceed on the assumption that the burden of proving a claim lies with whoever asserts it. As a result, she will make claims only if she is able to support them with evidence and logic. If someone else makes a claim, she will expect him to be able to support it in like fashion, and if he can't, she will dismiss the claim out of hand. If this dismissal is challenged, a Thinker will not invoke logic, law, or ethics in her defense. She will instead invoke the "economics of thinking." Allow me to explain.

If you are prudent, you will put yourself on multiple budgets. You will, for example, budget your income, making sure that you have enough to cover fixed expenses. You will also take care not to waste your income. You will likewise budget your time, spending it on rewarding activities and doing your best not to waste it. And finally, you will budget your thought. Thinking requires both time and energy, so you will be selective in what you think about. This is one of the reasons a Thinker is quick to dismiss theories that aren't falsifiable. Such theories, she knows, are useless for making predictions and are therefore a waste of her brainpower.

Suppose, then, that a Thinker encounters someone making an unorthodox claim. She might be willing to hear the person out. She is, after all, open-minded, and she knows that many claims that are now regarded as common sense were at one time unorthodox. After hearing the claim, though, she will ask what evidence the person has in support of it. If he refuses to answer this question, if he admits to having no evidence, or if the evidence he has is implausible, she will quickly lose interest in the claim.

At this point, the claimer might attempt to shift the burden of proof onto the Thinker's shoulders: "Can you *disprove* my claim? If you can't, it is incumbent on you to accept what I am saying!" The Thinker will not fall for this ruse. She knows that were she to adopt this principle, she would end up spending vast amounts of her precious thinking time disproving unsubstantiated claims. She also knows that were she to go to the trouble of disproving one of this person's claims, there is nothing to stop him from coming up with another unsupported claim for her to disprove, followed by another. After all, it takes a lot less effort to make claims than it does to disprove them.

The burden-of-proof issue arises with respect to religion. Because theists claim that God exists, it is intellectually incumbent on them to provide supporting evidence, which can be tricky.

Similarly, because atheists claim that God doesn't exist, it is also incumbent on them to come up with supporting evidence, which again can be tricky. Agnostics, however, make no claims regarding God's existence: "Maybe he does, maybe he doesn't. I don't know." They are therefore unencumbered by any burden of proof.

The advent of the internet has made it easy for bad actors to pollute the information space with outlandish claims. (I will have much more to say about this phenomenon in a later chapter.) Many people feel drowned by the resulting flood of mis- and disinformation. They don't know what to believe and what not to believe. They would therefore do well to follow in the footsteps of the Thinker and employ the burden-of-proof concept as their primary filter for the online claims people make. If you encounter an amazing claim, but the person making it is unwilling or unable to provide evidence in support of it, you should simply ignore it. You have better things to think about!

4 | Inconsistent Beliefs

A set of beliefs is inconsistent if it is impossible for them all to be true. If someone tells us that he believes that Bigfoot exists, we might respond by asking for evidence in support of this belief; likewise, if he tells us that he believes that Bigfoot doesn't exist. Suppose, however, that someone tells us he *both* believes that Bigfoot exists *and* believes that he doesn't exist. It is logically impossible for both beliefs to be true. We can therefore conclude, without doing any research, that one of them is false. We may not know which it is, but we know that one of them must be. This is why it is so intellectually satisfying to catch someone in an inconsistency. You don't need to do research to refute them. You need only invoke logic.

If we encountered such a person, we might ask him to elaborate on his beliefs regarding Bigfoot. Suppose he explains that although he believes that Bigfoot exists *in people's minds*, he doesn't believe that Bigfoot exists *in the actual world*. We would then conclude that despite appearances to the contrary, he isn't guilty of inconsistency; he is just sloppy in his use of language. If, however, he tells us that he both believes that Bigfoot exists in the actual world and believes that Bigfoot doesn't exist in the actual world, and adds that he isn't joking, we can legitimately question his rationality.

If inconsistencies were always this blatant, we could easily detect and avoid them. The problem is that inconsistent beliefs can be subtle, meaning that we can be oblivious to their presence within us. Indeed, there is an excellent chance that you harbor such beliefs. Later in this chapter, we will look for them.

Inconsistency Explored

The above case involves an inconsistent *pair* of statements. This is the most blatant kind of inconsistency. It is also possible, though, for a *triplet* of statements to be inconsistent:

Socrates is a man.
All men are mortal.
Socrates is immortal.

Although any two of these statements can simultaneously be true, they can't all three be true. If we encountered someone who held these three beliefs, we might therefore try to talk sense into him: "Think about it. If Socrates is a man and all men are mortal, then Socrates would have to be mortal, right? But you believe that he is *im*mortal." The triplet of claims is therefore inconsistent but not as blatantly inconsistent as the pair of claims that Bigfoot both exists and doesn't exist.

If the person who holds these three beliefs responds by abandoning his belief that Socrates is immortal, the inconsistency is resolved. Other resolutions are possible, though. He can instead continue to believe that all men are mortal and that Socrates is immortal, but give up the belief that Socrates is a man. He will, of course, be left with the challenge of supporting the belief that Socrates is not a man, but he will have resolved the inconsistency. Alternatively, he can continue to believe that Socrates is a man and that Socrates is immortal, but give up the belief that all men are mortal. Again, the inconsistency will have been resolved.

Inconsistencies can be even more involved than this. Consider, for example, the following set of twenty-six mathematical assertions: $a < b, b < c, c < d, \ldots, y < z$, and $z < a$. Although any two of these assertions—indeed any twenty-five of them[1]—will be consistent, the whole set can't be; at least one of these assertions must be mistaken. Generally speaking, the larger a belief set is, the more likely it is to harbor inconsistencies.

Realize that there is a difference between *inconsistency* and *hypocrisy*. Whereas an inconsistent person holds beliefs that cannot all be true, a hypocrite behaves in a manner that is at odds with his stated beliefs.[2] (Suppose, for example, that a prominent environmentalist insists on traveling to his speaking engagements in a private jet.) Whereas inconsistency is evidence of a logical shortcoming, hypocrisy is generally taken to be evidence of a character flaw or moral shortcoming. This is why the accusation of being a hypocrite stings more than the accusation of being inconsistent.

It is also important to distinguish between what might be called *synchronous* and *asynchronous* inconsistency. In the former, we hold, *at a given point in time*, beliefs that cannot all be true. The person who told us that he currently believes both that

Bigfoot exists and that Bigfoot doesn't exist is guilty of synchronous inconsistency. Suppose, though, that a person who used to believe that Bigfoot exists changes his mind and comes to believe that Bigfoot does not exist. This is an example of *asynchronous* inconsistency: His current beliefs are inconsistent with his former beliefs. Ralph Waldo Emerson is famously quoted as saying that "consistency is the hobgoblin of little minds." While it is true that he wrote these words, it is useful to consider the context in which they appear:

> A *foolish* [emphasis added] consistency is the hobgoblin of little minds, adored by little statesmen and philosophers and divines. With consistency a great soul has simply nothing to do. He may as well concern himself with his shadow on the wall. Speak what you think now in hard words, and to-morrow speak what to-morrow thinks in hard words again, though it contradict everything you said to-day.[3]

It is clear that in this passage, Emerson is deriding synchronous rather than asynchronous inconsistency.

As a highly rational person, a Thinker will be anxious to avoid synchronous inconsistency, but she will have no problem with asynchronous inconsistency. She knows that anyone who criticizes her for disbelieving today what she believed yesterday is basically criticizing her for being open-minded enough to change her beliefs in response to new information. This is a trait, however, that she is proud to possess, meaning that she will find it easy to dismiss such criticisms. Furthermore, although a Thinker values synchronous consistency, she knows that the mere fact that your beliefs are consistent isn't necessarily something to boast about. They could, after all, be consistently mistaken!

The (Latent) Inconsistency of Absolute Pacifism

A Thinker is unlikely to fall victim to blatant inconsistency, such as believing both that Bigfoot exists and doesn't exist (in the actual world). There is a very good chance, though, that subtle inconsistencies lurk in her belief set. To get a better understanding of this phenomenon, let us turn our attention to the beliefs of an absolute pacifist.

Whereas mainstream pacifists oppose violence as a means of settling disputes, absolute pacifists believe that "it is wrong always, everywhere, for anyone, to use violence against another human being."[4] If asked to defend this position, an absolute pacifist might point to the preciousness of human life. In doing so, however, he is opening himself to the charge of inconsistency. To see why, let's perform a thought experiment: Suppose a terrorist is about to detonate a backpack bomb on a crowded street. If he detonates it, he will be killed, along with dozens of other people. If the police shoot him before he detonates the bomb, though, only he will be killed. (And in case you are wondering, no, the police can't stop him by just wounding him, since on hearing gunfire, he would immediately detonate the bomb.) Under these circumstances, the terrorist is going to die for sure; the only question is whether he dies from a police bullet or from the bomb he is carrying. If life is indeed precious, shouldn't the police shoot the terrorist, inasmuch as doing so would minimize the loss of life? In fact, wouldn't it be not just morally *permissible* but morally *obligatory* for them to shoot the terrorist?

This story is admittedly far-fetched, and for all I know, the situation I have described has never occurred. But because the absolute pacifist is making such a strong claim—that *under every conceivable state of affairs* it is wrong to kill a human being—all that is needed to refute him is an internally consistent story in which it *would* be morally permissible to do so. The backpack bomber story fits the bill. And how would an absolute pacifist respond to this story? If he tells us that under these circumstances it would be permissible to kill the terrorist, he will be abandoning his absolutism. If he instead tells us that it would be impermissible to kill the terrorist, he would appear to be abandoning the claim on which his absolute pacifism is based—namely, that life is "precious."

It is tempting to adopt absolutist positions with respect to moral issues by claiming that an action is, *without exception*, morally impermissible. By taking this stand, we project an image of being in some sense "morally pure." From our pedestal, we can look down on those who disagree with us as being somehow morally compromised. Another benefit of taking absolutist positions is that doing so allows us to sidestep difficult cases. From our point of view, all instances of killing would simply be wrong—end of discussion.

Absolutism comes with a downside, though. Because absolutist claims are so strong, and because the world is a complicated place, such claims are typically difficult to defend. For this reason, Thinkers will be reluctant to take absolutist positions, preferring instead to take nuanced positions: "Is killing wrong? It depends on the circumstances." If requested, she will then spell out those circumstances. Yes, doing so will require intellectual effort, but it is the price that must be paid if her goal is not simply to look morally pure but to fill her mind with true beliefs.

The inconsistency of simultaneously believing that Bigfoot exists and believing that he doesn't exist is a *blatant* inconsistency, one that jumps out at us. This is not the case, however, with simultaneously believing that life is precious and believing that it would be wrong to kill the suicide bomber. This second inconsistency might therefore be characterized as *latent*, and in much the same way as a latent fingerprint left at a crime scene must be developed to become visible, a latent inconsistency must be "developed" to become apparent. Whereas crime detectives might use powders to reveal latent fingerprints, philosophers tell stories—like the one about the suicide bomber—to reveal latent inconsistencies. In a moment, I will tell another story that might reveal a latent inconsistency that readers unwittingly harbor.

Cockfighting Reconsidered

Have you ever been to a cockfight? Probably not. I haven't either, but I've come close. On a trip to Cuba, I was surprised when, during a tour of a tobacco plantation, our guide showed us what he described as "the cockpit." I was puzzled as we obviously weren't in an airplane. The cockpit, he explained, is where they fight cocks. In response to my still-puzzled look, he said, "Cocks—you know, boy chickens."

In many parts of the world, people fight "boy chickens," but calling them "chickens" is likely to summon up the wrong mental image. The creatures that come to mind are docile, unathletic, and overweight. The gamecocks used in cockfights, by way of contrast, are not far removed from their junglefowl ancestors. They have magnificent plumage, are supremely fit, and are quite aggressive toward any other gamecock that might be present. In a cockfight, two gamecocks are placed into an enclosed cockpit where they fight to the death, with the last bird standing declared the winner. People watch these fights, both for entertainment and as a vehicle for betting.

In my critical thinking courses, we would typically spend a lecture talking about cockfighting. After explaining what it involved, I would ask for a show of hands: "How many of you think cockfighting is morally wrong?" In a typical group, nearly every hand would go up. When I asked why they felt this way, they might point to the needless suffering it inflicts on animals.

Having set my students up in this manner, I would let the other shoe drop by changing the subject from gamecocks to the chickens known as *broilers*. I would explain that "broiler" is the commercial term for the chickens they buy in stores and restaurants. (Even if the chicken in question is fried or roasted instead of broiled, it counts as a broiler.) I would then ask for another show of hands: "How many of you have eaten meat from a broiler in the last week?" Most hands would rise, but it became apparent that some of the more thoughtful students were getting nervous about my line of questioning.

I would then describe the lives of gamecocks and broilers. Those who breed and raise gamecocks generally take very good care of them. The birds grow up in a fairly natural environment and are given quality food, as well as food supplements. To develop their fighting ability, they are allowed to spar with other gamecocks, but to prevent sparring injuries, their spurs are trimmed. When they reach their prime, maybe at age two, these trimmed spurs are supplemented with sharp metal blades, and the birds are fought.

Whereas gamecocks are bred and raised to be strong and aggressive, broilers are bred and raised to be docile and to gain weight quickly. Instead of having the magnificent plumage of their junglefowl ancestors, they might have short white feathers. They emerge from their eggshell in commercial hatcheries. They never meet the mothers with which, in the wild or even in a farmyard, they would spend the first month or two of their life. They are instead dumped together into the large indoor pens of what are known as *broiler farms*.

At first there is lots of space between birds, but as they grow, conditions become increasingly congested. There is little for them to do but eat, drink, and be bored. In this crowded and stressful environment, birds get sick, but instead of being cared for, they are left to die. Their droppings also accumulate, meaning that they live in their own waste, exposed to both microbes and to a noxious level of ammonia. Because of their rapid growth, their legs might be too weak for them to walk, and their heart and lungs are barely up to the task of keeping them alive.

After a month or two of this existence, the broilers are big enough to be "harvested." They are grabbed, stuffed into cages with many other birds, and loaded onto the trucks that will transport them to the slaughterhouse. On this ride they might see the sun and breathe fresh air for the first time in their short life, but rather than being exhilarated by the experience, they are likely to be confused and even terrified: It is so different than their previous environment! On arriving at their destination, they are removed from their cages and hung by their feet on a kind of conveyer belt. Their throats are mechanically slit, and their bodies fall into scalding water to set the stage for feather removal.

On completing my presentation about the lives of broilers, I would ask for another show of hands: "How many of you think broiler farming is morally wrong?" Some hands would go up, but the classroom atmosphere had clearly changed. At this point, I would do one final poll: "Remind me, how many of you have eaten meat from a broiler in the last week?" The distress of some of the students was palpable.

Enter the Mysterious Stranger

The absolute pacifist, as we have seen, harbored a latent inconsistency in his belief set. In their beliefs regarding cruelty to animals, however, many of my students also appear to harbor a latent inconsistency. They think it is morally wrong to cause animals to suffer, and for this reason, they condemn cockfighting. At the same time, they have few qualms about eating broilers, even though a compelling case can be made that broilers suffer more than gamecocks.

To "develop" the inconsistency of the absolute pacifist, I told a story about a suicide bomber. To similarly develop the inconsistency in many of my students' beliefs about the morality of cockfighting and broiler farming, I would tell a rather different story. Imagine that reincarnation is true. Imagine, in other words, that when you die, you will come back, but in a different body. It might be the body of a different person who is born shortly after you die, but it might also be the body of a cow or even a beetle. It will, in other words, be like the reincarnation envisioned by Hindus.

Now imagine that while on a Sunday evening walk, you encounter a mysterious stranger wearing sunglasses, a fedora, and a trench coat. He comes up and announces that he is the bearer of bad news: You are going to die in the near future. He makes it clear that this isn't a threat and in particular that *he* isn't going to kill you. He is simply informing you of your impending demise and goes on to explain that there is nothing you can do to prevent it. You are astonished and tell him that you don't believe a word of what he says. He sighs: "Most people respond to my visits this way. But take this list and think about what I have said. If you want to talk some more—and hear some good news—be here at this time on Friday." He hands you an envelope, after which he dissolves into nothingness before your very eyes.

You find yourself questioning whether what happened actually happened, but you hold in your hand physical evidence that the event was real. You open the envelope to find a paper that, for each of the next four days, lists a person's name along with a brief description of how that person is going to die. On Monday morning, you start doing research on the people in question. The first person listed turns out to be a prominent politician in the Republic of Nauru. She will, the list says, die in a motorcycle accident. Late on Monday you again enter her name in a search engine to do more research, only to encounter news that she has died in a rather improbable accident involving the motorcycle she was driving and a land crab. On Tuesday morning, you turn your attention to the second person on the list, who turns out to be an Indian pop-star. Later that day, you look for more information about him, only to learn that he has been trampled to death by a rogue elephant, the way the list said he would. The list, you conclude, is not some kind of sick joke. It should instead be taken very seriously.

On Wednesday morning, you research the third name. He turns out to be a renegade American politician. The list says that an extremist using a blowgun dart tipped in curare is going to attack him. You try to contact this politician to warn him, only to be rebuffed by "his people." You call the police to warn them, but they just laugh at you. Late on Wednesday, though, the news carries reports of his assassination—you guessed it, by a curare-tipped dart shot from a blowgun.

On Thursday morning, you turn to your list, determined to prevent the predicted death. The fourth person is listed simply as "John Smith, Springfield, USA." According to the list, he will die as a result of getting struck by lightning while working on his chimney cap. You realize that because there are lots of John Smiths and lots of Springfields in America, it is hopeless to intervene, so you let fate take its course. Late on Thursday, you do an internet search for "John Smith Springfield," only to learn that a person named John Smith in Springfield, Ohio, has died as a result of getting struck by lightning while working on his chimney cap.

Come Friday, you are convinced that the mysterious stranger has the power to foretell people's deaths, and you resolve to meet him again that evening to ask questions and hear the good news he had mentioned. You go to the appropriate place at the appropriate time, but no one is there. You stand waiting, and your heart is starting to sink, when you feel a tapping on your shoulder. You turn around, and there he is, the mysterious stranger (MS) you previously encountered. The following conversation ensues:

MS: I thought you would be back.
YOU: Okay, I believe you, but I've got some questions.
MS: Let me guess. You want to know if there is anything you can do to prevent your death. The answer, unfortunately, is that there isn't.
YOU: Alright, but can you at least tell me when and how I will die?
MS: Nope. That would be against their rules. And in case you are wondering, no, I can't tell you who "they" are.
YOU: Alright, alright! But when we met on Sunday, you said you had both good and bad news for me. You've given me the bad news—namely, that I will soon die—but what's the good news?
MS: The good news is that after you die, you not only will be reincarnated but get to choose what you come back as.
YOU: I don't like having to die, but given that I do, this *is* good news. Basically, I want to come back as someone who is going to be brilliant and good looking. Also, it would be nice to have parents who are both loving and rich.
MS: Sorry, but it doesn't work that way. In your case, the reincarnation powers-that-be have decided that because of the way you have lived your life, you will come back as either a gamecock or a commercially raised broiler. They have also decided to let you choose. Lucky you! So which will it be?

At this point I would ask my students what *their* choice would be: Would they come back as a gamecock or a broiler? The vast majority typically chose to come back as a gamecock. When asked why, they might respond along these lines: "It's a better life. Yes, the end is violent, but at least I would get to fight for my life. Also, the life that precedes it is one of the best lives my chicken-self could have."

"Then isn't it," I would ask, "inconsistent for you to condemn cockfighting while supporting, with your food purchases, the commercial production of broilers?"

Dealing with Double Standards

By challenging my students in the manner described, I was in effect accusing them of having a double standard. Although they opposed the cruelty involved in cockfighting, they were complicit in the even worse cruelty involved in the commercial production of broilers. Many of them, I could sense, did not appreciate my efforts, so I would make amends by laying out the ways in which they could defend themselves against my imputations.

Option 1: They could abandon the principle that it is morally wrong to cause animals to suffer needlessly. No student ever chose this option, but if one had, I would have used it as an opportunity to explore his moral beliefs as well as his beliefs regarding cruelty. It would have been an interesting conversation.

Option 2: They could challenge my account of the treatment of gamecocks and broilers. They might, in particular, claim that broilers weren't treated as badly as I had said. This also never happened in my classes, but if it had, I would have asked those who made this claim for supporting evidence and would have offered them class time in which to present their evidence to the group. I would subsequently have presented my own evidence, and we would have discussed the matter.

Option 3: Students could continue to condemn needless cruelty to animals and admit that my account of the lives of gamecocks and broilers was correct, but they could point to what they took to be a morally significant difference between the treatment of gamecocks and the treatment of broilers. One such response: "People fight gamecocks for fun, because they enjoy watching them fight. We don't raise and eat broilers for fun, though. We eat them to meet our nutritional needs." In other words, they would admit that broilers are treated cruelly but deny that the cruelty in question was *needless* cruelty; rather, our health required it.

I would offer a three-part response to this assertion. First, those who eat broilers typically do so "for fun": They eat chicken because they like the way it tastes; indeed, if they disliked chicken, they probably wouldn't eat it, even if their doctor advised them to do so. Second, the lives of vegans and vegetarians demonstrate that we don't need to eat chicken or eat meat in general to stay healthy. In fact, the medical consensus seems to be that the less meat we eat, the better.[5] Third, suppose I am mistaken and we *do* need to eat chickens to stay healthy. We could do so without causing them so much suffering. We could, in particular, let them have long lives in a natural environment before killing them in a humane manner. It is currently possible to buy and consume these "pasture-raised" chickens, as they are called, but it will cost more and be somewhat inconvenient to do so: Not every grocery carries meat from such chickens, and few restaurants offer it. If you were really opposed to causing needless suffering to animals, though, wouldn't this inconvenience and extra expense be a price worth paying? And if you refuse to pay it, aren't you guilty of hypocrisy?

Double standards thrive in an environment awash in misinformation and missing information. If you have no idea how broilers are raised, it is easy to assume that they are not treated cruelly. It might even be possible for you to believe, as many consumers appear to, that hatchling chickens are somehow magically transformed into the shrink-wrapped chicken body parts sold in supermarkets. It is also easy for a person who has developed a taste for chicken not to ask questions about how the chickens he eats are raised—and to resent it when some annoying philosophy prof nevertheless tells him.

Option 4: Students could stop treating gamecocks and broilers differently. There are two ways to do this:

Option 4a: Instead of claiming that it is morally wrong to fight gamecocks but morally permissible to treat broilers the way we do, they could admit that *both* activities are morally wrong. Do this, and the double standard will disappear—as will chicken for dinner!

Option 4b: Instead of morally condemning the treatment of broilers, they could condone cockfighting. In other words, they could maintain that fighting gamecocks and raising broilers were *both* morally permissible activities. Do this, and they would once again stop treating the two groups of chickens differently. Choosing this option, however, would be tantamount to abandoning the principle that it is morally wrong to cause animals to suffer needlessly, in which case I would respond the same as if they had chosen Option 1.

So, which of the above options did my students choose? Most chose none of them, at least not then and there. They instead responded to my challenge by putting the whole matter "on hold." In some cases, they assumed that, with a bit of effort, they would be able to come up with a morally significant difference between fighting gamecocks and commercially raising broilers. In other cases, they would go away hoping that, with the passage of time, they would simply forget the issues I had raised. Some readers might, at this point, be tempted to follow their example.

Why Are We Inconsistent?

To better understand our susceptibility to inconsistency, consider again the belief-acquisition process. Your belief set, as we have seen, is enormous. It is therefore impractical for you, in the course of daily life, to pause to consider whether a potential new belief is consistent with all your current beliefs. As a result, you are likely to adopt beliefs that are inconsistent with those beliefs— maybe latently inconsistent, but inconsistent nonetheless. Indeed, it would be amazing if you didn't harbor any inconsistent beliefs!

If you are in the habit of making sweeping generalizations, you dramatically increase your chances of harboring inconsistent beliefs. Consider again the absolute pacifist who believed both that life is precious and that it is never, under any circumstances, morally permissible to kill another person. We saw that although these two beliefs might appear to be consistent, they are in fact inconsistent, albeit in a subtle manner.

We often harbor inconsistent beliefs as a result of our upbringing. Thus, the parents who taught you that it is wrong to be cruel to animals might have routinely fed you chicken. As a result, you quite understandably assumed that the chickens you enjoyed at dinner had not been treated cruelly; otherwise, your seemingly all-knowing parents would not have fed them to you. Later in life, you might have come across a video showing gamecocks fighting to the death. You likely would have been disgusted by the apparent bloodlust of the spectators. You might also have assumed that the birds that died in this cruel manner had been cruelly mistreated while alive. As a result, the two prongs of your double standard would be in place. You would be convinced that although it is morally wrong to fight chickens, there is nothing wrong with eating them.

Notice that which double standards you acquire will, to a considerable extent, depend on your culture. Had you been raised in Vietnam, you might grow up thinking that fighting gamecocks was as morally permissible as eating chickens, which in turn was as morally permissible as eating dogs.[6] Had you been born in first-century CE Rome, you would likely think that eating chickens was as morally permissible as forcing gamecocks to fight to the death, which in turn was as morally permissible as forcing slaves, prisoners of war, and criminals to do the same.

We smugly look at other cultures and even our ancestors and are astonished by their moral depravity. Eating crickets and rats? Disgusting! Eating dogs? More disgusting still! Entertaining themselves by watching enslaved people engage in mortal combat? An abomination! We should keep in mind, though, that other cultures are also astonished by what they regard as evidence of our moral depravity. Realize, too, that it is not only possible but likely that our descendants will similarly look back on us in disgust: "Really? They raised intelligent animals like pigs in horrifying conditions[7] and subsequently slaughtered them just because they enjoyed the taste of bacon? What *were* they thinking?" Or who knows, maybe they will be astonished that we would be disgusted by the thought of eating a medium-rare chimpanzee steak.

A Thinker knows how easy it is to acquire inconsistent beliefs. She also knows that once acquired, inconsistencies can lurk in a person's belief set for years or even decades without being recognized for what they are. She will therefore assume that she harbors multiple inconsistencies and will set about trying to find and eradicate them, but in doing so, she will quickly encounter a major hindrance in the form of her ego. It will assure her that there are no inconsistencies to be found, and should she be presented with evidence of one, her ego will encourage her to ignore it. If this strategy fails, her ego will help her rationalize the inconsistency. That's the bad news.

The good news is that other people have egos as well. Yes, these egos blind them to their shortcomings but at the same time make them acutely aware of other people's shortcomings. This is part of their ego's strategy for making them feel superior to those around them. This means that other people can play an important role in helping a Thinker discover and overcome her shortcomings and, in particular, her inconsistent beliefs. To avail herself of this valuable free service, though, she will have to rein in her defensive tendencies. When accused of inconsistency, she will have to make a point of hearing out her accusers and thinking carefully about their accusations.

Once she becomes aware of an apparent inconsistency in her belief set, a Thinker might experience what psychologists refer to as *cognitive dissonance*. She will be annoyed by its presence there, and until she resolves it, she will experience the intellectual equivalent of walking with a pebble in her shoe: It is possible to keep walking, but it is uncomfortable to do so, and the farther you walk, the more uncomfortable you become.

Some readers might at this point be experiencing the pebble-in-the-shoe phenomenon with respect to eating broilers, so an admission is in order. The pebble I have attempted to put in your shoe used to be in my shoe. It resided there for a decade before I properly dealt with it. Feel free to pass it on.

PART II

Word Problems

5 | Ambiguous Words

As we have seen, putting a belief into words will be difficult if the belief is fuzzy or empty. Even if we know exactly what we believe, though, the ambiguity of language can make it difficult to share our beliefs with others.

People talk about *the* definition of a word, even though it is almost never the case that a word has only one definition.[1] By way of illustration, consider the very simple sentence "Cats sit." One dictionary[2] gives seven different definitions of "cat," used as a noun, including *a kind of animal*, *a malicious woman*, and *a devotee of jazz*. The same dictionary gives eight different definitions of "sit," used as a verb, including *resting on one's buttocks*, *covering eggs*, and *posing for a portrait.* As a consequence, "Cats sit" can mean 7 × 8 = 56 different things, including that malicious women cover eggs and that devotees of jazz pose for portraits. (That's a lot of possible meanings but realize that the sentence "Cats run" can mean 4,515 different things![3]) Nevertheless, when those fluent in English read "Cats sit," they instantly and unconsciously assume that the writer is asserting that kitty cats rest on their buttocks. This is a remarkable but easily overlooked linguistic ability.

The written sentence "Cats sit" may have fifty-six different meanings, but the spoken sentence has even more. This is because we can use inflection to put a spin on the meanings of the words we utter. Consider, for example, the lone word "really," said in response to a claim. Depending on our intonation, it can be a vigorous affirmation of that claim, an expression of doubt regarding the claim, or an expression of surprise on hearing it. Because written words lack intonation, it can be hard to discern sarcasm in written communication. Suppose you send someone a video of something you were astounded by, and they respond with the text message "Wow." Are they also astounded, or is it a sarcastic "wow"? It's hard to tell—unless their one word is accompanied by emojis.

The ambiguity of language can undermine sincere attempts at communication. Suppose, for example, that the parties to a conversation are inadvertently using the same word in two different ways and, as a result, find themselves talking past each other. A sense of frustration will soon set in—"Why can't she understand the point I am trying to make?"—which in turn can bring the conversation to a premature and unsatisfactory conclusion.

The Uses of Ambiguity

Some people exploit the ambiguity of language to create puns. I happen to be one of them: "When does a joke become a 'dad joke'? When it becomes apparent."[4] The ambiguity of language has other, less amusing uses, though. A debater, for example, might exploit ambiguity by equivocating: In the middle of a debate, he might intentionally switch the meaning of a key term to flummox his opponent. Along similar lines, a lawyer might include an ambiguous term in a contract and later interpret the ambiguity in a manner that benefits his client. To prevent this from happening, many legal systems adhere to the doctrine of *contra proferentem*: Ambiguities in a contract are to be interpreted in the manner that goes *against* the interests of the person who *drafted* it. This is part of the reason contracts are so wordy: The lawyers who draft them don't want there to be any ambiguities that the other party to the contract can exploit, and avoiding these ambiguities requires explanatory language. Another reason contracts are wordy, of course, is to deter the other party from reading them. Have you ever read your sixteen-thousand-word-long Microsoft services agreement? Me neither. And when the updated agreement comes in a few months, I probably won't read it either. And not to be forgotten, those who do not want you to read a contract, besides using very many words, might put those words in tiny print.

Ambiguity can also be used not to make people laugh but to sell them books. Philosopher Daniel Dennett has accused theologian Karen Armstrong of doing just this.[5] The title of her book *A History of God*, Dennett complains, is ambiguous because it leaves open the question of whether she is presenting a history of God *the being* or a history of *the concept of* God. The former history would presumably begin with God's creation of time itself—if such a thing were possible—followed by his creation of the universe, man, Jesus, and so on. It would also describe God's various interactions with humans. Armstrong's book doesn't do this, though. It instead spends its pages explaining the way *the God concept* has changed through human history. A case can be made, then, that her book would more accurately have been titled *A History of the Concept of God*—a title, one suspects, that would have attracted far fewer readers than the title under which the book was published. Dennett also complains that the book doesn't even offer a history of the concept of God. It instead uses "God" in an ambiguous manner, sometimes to refer to the concept of God and other times to refer to God the being. Having said this, I should add that Dennett himself has been accused of employing a similar tactic in choosing the title for his book, *Consciousness Explained*. A more accurate title, some critics complained, would have been *Consciousness Explained Away*.[6] Touché!

Ambiguous language is often a source of friction in relationships. Your significant other (SO), for example, might have told you that the dog leash was "in the car," but when you went out to get it, the leash wasn't there, so you went back into the house for clarification.

You: The leash isn't in the car.
SO: It *is* in the car. I purposely left it on the front seat of your car.
You: Oh, *my* car. Why didn't you say that in the first place?
SO: I did!
You: No, you said *the* car without specifying which one.
SO: You should have known that by saying *the* car I meant *your* car!

When we express ourselves to someone, we know what we are trying to say. The problem is that other people don't have direct access to our mind the way we do. All they have to go on is the words we write or speak, meaning that to communicate successfully, we must choose our words with care.

Ambiguous Questions

To better appreciate the problems caused by ambiguity, let us take a look at questions which, because of their ambiguity, are likely to give rise to pointless debate:

Is abortion wrong? Besides being contentious, this question is confusing because the word "wrong" is ambiguous: An act is *legally* wrong if it violates whatever the laws of the land happen to be; an act is *morally* wrong if it violates the "universal" laws of morality. The laws of the land are typically decided by whoever is in charge, and in many cases, those making the decision won't be particularly enlightened. For this reason, it is possible for an activity to be morally wrong but not legally wrong: Consider owning slaves in Mississippi in 1840. It is also possible for an activity to be legally wrong but not morally wrong: Consider interracial marriage in Mississippi in 1840.[7] On being asked whether abortion is wrong, then, a Thinker's first task will be to determine whether the questioner is talking about abortion being *legally* wrong or *morally* wrong.

Are men rude? This question is doubly ambiguous. By "men," does the questioner mean *all* men, *most* men, or *some* men? And in asking about their behavior, does he mean being rude *all* of the time, *much* of the time, or *some* of the time? If he is asking whether *all* men are *always* rude, the answer is, "Clearly not." If he is instead asking whether *some* men are *sometimes* rude, the answer is, "Of course." In response to this question, a Thinker might therefore ask for clarification, and while she as at it, she might also ask what, in the eyes of the questioner, constitutes rude behavior.

Is Islam a religion of violence? This question makes the mistake of treating Islam as a monolithic religion, when in fact there are different Islamic sects which themselves have subsects. Therefore, asking whether Islam is a religion of violence makes no more sense than asking whether animals have antlers: Some animals do, other animals don't. Suppose that in response to this criticism, the question is revised: "Is the Zaidiyyah branch of Shia Islam a religion of violence?" A Thinker might now respond by asking for a clarification of what constitutes a "religion of violence."

Are UFOs real? It depends on what you mean by "UFO."[8] It is the acronym for *unidentified flying object*, and if you ask whether such objects are real, the answer is that *of course* they are. Suppose, for example, that you notice, out of the corner of your eye, something moving through the air. You direct your gaze toward it, only to have it disappear behind a building. Was it a flying object? Yes. Can you identify it? No. It might have been a bird, a thrown object, a piece of paper blown by the wind, a balloon, a drone, or maybe even a craft piloted by alien beings, but you don't know which. For you, then, it will count as an unidentified flying object—which might or might not be an alien spacecraft. Establishing this last claim would require more evidence.

During my life, I have seen many flying objects that I could not identify, but I doubt that any of them were alien spacecraft. Indeed, elsewhere I have argued that although intelligent beings almost certainly exist elsewhere in the universe, it is highly unlikely that they are visiting Earth.[9]

Is evolution "just a theory"? Like the words "cat" and "sit," the word "theory" has multiple meanings. It can refer to *a hypothesis assumed for the sake of argument or investigation*. Suppose, for example, that George can't find his credit card. "My theory," he might tell us, "is that I somehow left it at the restaurant." He might add that he is by no means sure that this is what happened—that for him, it is "just a theory." Evolution is not a theory in this sense of the word. It is instead *a plausible or scientifically acceptable general principle or body of principles offered to explain phenomena.* Any biologist will be able not only to explain the theory of evolution but to provide support for it. Consequently, it is misleading to describe the theory of evolution as being "just a theory."

What is the unemployment rate? A Thinker will likely respond to this question with a question of her own: "You talk about *the* unemployment rate, but there isn't one rate, there are several. Which are you talking about?" If the questioner seems puzzled, she might go on to describe some of the ways in which "unemployment" can be defined:

- An unemployed^1 person is someone who lacks a job. [Note: I am adding numerical superscripts to these definitions to facilitate subsequent discussion.]
- An unemployed^2 person is someone who lacks a job but wants one.
- An unemployed^3 person is someone who lacks a job, and who not only wants one but is actively seeking one.

Most people would say that the first of these is the obvious definition: To be unemployed is to not be employed; to be unemployed, in other words, is to lack a job. The US government, however, typically relies on the third definition: To count as unemployed, you must not only lack a job and want one, but you must be actively seeking one. This has the effect of making the "unemployment" rate much lower than it would be under the first or second definition. Notice, in particular, that people who have been unemployed so long that they have given up on finding a job will count as unemployed[1] and might count as unemployed[2] as well, but they will not count as unemployed[3] and will therefore not show up on the official unemployment statistics. As a result, at the depths of a particularly brutal recession, when the number of unemployed[2] people is at all-time highs, the official unemployment rate might be remarkably low because people will stop looking for employment that obviously isn't available.[10] Politicians and administrators are not above exploiting the ambiguity of language and might creatively "redefine" words to make themselves look better. Lots of people will be fooled by this maneuver, but a Thinker won't.

What is the poverty rate? A Thinker might again respond to this question with a question—"What do you mean by *poverty*?"—and might go on to describe some of the ways in which a person can be impoverished:

- An *economically* impoverished person has insufficient income and wealth, typically resulting in insufficient food, clothing, and shelter.
- An *intellectually* impoverished person lacks an education, resulting in impaired thinking ability and diminished job prospects.
- A *culturally* impoverished person lacks an understanding of his culture, resulting in an inability to appreciate it.
- A *spiritually* impoverished person lacks a feeling of connection to God.

- A *socially* impoverished person lacks meaningful social relationships.

Most people, when they talk about poverty, have economic poverty in mind. To their way of thinking, this is the kind of poverty that matters most. Not everyone shares these values, though. A Cistercian monk, for example, is more likely to be concerned with spiritual poverty and might therefore pity a person who, although a billionaire, lacks a connection to God. Likewise, an elderly person's primary concern might be to avoid becoming socially impoverished. Suppose, then, that in response to our request for clarification, the person rephrases his question: "What is the *economic* poverty rate?" Even this revised question is ambiguous, though, since there are many different ways to measure economic poverty.[11]

A Thinker will be cognizant of the disruptive role ambiguity plays in human communication. Should it become apparent that she and whomever she is talking to are on different linguistic tracks, she might pause for clarification: "Oh, you are talking about *material* poverty. I was talking about *spiritual* poverty." She realizes, however, that many non-Thinkers have little tolerance for such clarification. To them, the Thinker's insistence that terms be clarified before a conversation continues might come across as pedantic behavior. Alternatively, they might think she is merely splitting linguistic hairs in an attempt to avoid discussing the issue at hand. She also knows that her attempts at disambiguation might have little impact on the other person's subsequent comments. As a result, in conversations with non-Thinkers she will walk on a linguistic tightrope, engaging in some but not too much linguistic clarification.

Repurposing Words

As we have seen, words generally have multiple definitions, which can frustrate our attempts to communicate: We use a word to mean one thing, but those who hear us assume that we have a different meaning in mind. Additional problems arise, however, when people "repurpose" words. Allow me to explain.

To be shared, concepts need names, and the nomenclator has two options. The first is to *invent* a word. Scientists routinely do this—think about "electron," "x-ray," and "photosynthesis." I did it myself a few chapters back when I invented the word "nonbelieve" to signify cases in which a person neither believes a claim to be true nor believes it to be false. Another way to name a concept is to *repurpose* an already existing word by assigning a new meaning to it. By way of illustration, the word "species" had been around for centuries before biologists started using it to designate a group of organisms that can interbreed and produce fertile offspring in nature. I similarly adopted the word "disbelieve" to refer to cases in which a person actively believes a claim to be false. Had I not taken this step, readers might misinterpret the claims I was making about disbelief, such as that from the mere fact that you don't believe something, it doesn't follow that you disbelieve it (because you might instead nonbelieve it).

Repurposing words can give rise to linguistic confusion. Suppose, for example, that before delivering a lecture about racism, a sociologist informs her (academic) audience that in her remarks she won't be using "racism" in the usual way, to refer simply to prejudice against members of a certain race; she will instead use it to refer to a particular kind of prejudice—namely, by people *in positions of power* against members of a certain race. For her purposes, then, "racism" will mean *prejudice plus power*.[12] As a result, when she subsequently asserts that it is impossible for, say, homeless Black people to be racist (because they aren't in positions of power), her audience won't be surprised. This conclusion, after all, is a direct consequence of the way she has chosen to use the word "racism."

So far, so good, but if she makes the same claim to her (nonacademic) relatives, they will be astonished and might offer an obvious counterexample: "What if homeless Black people went around saying that all white people are evil. Surely they would count as racist!" This disagreement is the result of people using the same word to mean different things, with the relatives relying on the *lexical* (dictionary) definition of "racism" and the sociologist relying on the *stipulative* definition that she has developed. As a result, they will talk past each other. When a Thinker hears someone—particularly in an academic environment—make what sounds like an outlandish or even ridiculous claim, she will pause to consider the possibility that this person has lapsed into jargon and will ask for clarification.

Invent a word, and you "own" it: The word can mean whatever you want. Repurpose an already-existing word, though, and your "lexical rights" will be limited. In particular, you don't have it in your power to eliminate the other definitions of the word. You also don't have it in your power to declare yours to be the best definition—or more boldly, the *correct* definition. Like it or not, it is just one of many definitions of the word.[13]

There is a good chance that as part of her self-education, a Thinker has read George Orwell's novel *Nineteen Eighty-Four*. As a result, she will be skeptical of attempts to improve language by putting "experts" in charge of the meanings of words. She knows that by controlling the language, they will be able to control what we can say, which in turn will have an impact on what we can think. She is much more comfortable living in a "linguistic democracy," in which the language is shaped only by the word usage of members of the linguistic community. Yes, the resulting language will be imperfect, and as a result there will be lots of miscommunication, but it will be the least bad of our linguistic options.

6 | Emotive Language

Ambiguity, as we have seen, can get in the way of communication: It can derail a discussion by causing people to talk past each other. Besides wasting time, this can make future discussions unlikely because each party will assume that the other party, by failing to understand what they have to say, is being stubbornly obtuse. This, however, is only one of many problems that arise when we use language.

Besides one word having two meanings, two words can have the same meaning. Consider, for example, "home" and "residence." Although the dictionary lists them as synonyms, these words are likely to evoke different emotions in those who hear them: Whereas "home" evokes feelings of warmth and belonging, "residence" feels impersonal. (Consider the difference between saying "Home, sweet home" and saying "Residence, sweet residence.") Likewise, although the dictionary lists "cheap" and "affordable" as synonyms, a person who takes pride in telling people that his car provides affordable transportation might be offended to hear someone characterize it as being cheap. And finally, although used cars have been around since the late 1800s, "pre-owned" cars came on the scene in the late 1990s.[1] By rebranding their used cars as pre-owned, dealers could increase the amount people were willing to pay for them.

To share our ideas with others, we must use words, but we have considerable leeway in which words we use. We can, in particular, use words that make the listener's heart and gut take an interest in what we are saying, which in turn can help us persuade them. Thus, in the early 1980s, the group that had described itself as being *anti-abortion* started using the term *pro-life*, and the group that had described itself as being pro-abortion started using the term *pro-choice*.[2] The beliefs of these two groups hadn't changed. They simply came to realize that the words we use, by affecting how we feel, affect what we believe, and they accomplished their linguistic rebranding by replacing the disagreeable word "abortion" with two upbeat words, "choice" and "life."

By Triggering Our Emotions, Words Can Disrupt Our Thought Processes

Is it wrong for teachers to discriminate in the classroom? Many readers will likely respond in the affirmative: "Of course it is!" This, at any rate, is how many of my students responded when I would ask them during group discussions. A case can be made, though, that discrimination is not only permissible in the classroom but in some cases is morally obligatory. Allow me to explain.

The word "discriminate" is ambiguous. On the one hand, it can mean *unfairly treat a person or group of people differently from other people or groups*. To keep things clear, let us refer to this as *discriminate*[1]. To *discriminate*[2], on the other hand, is to *distinguish by discerning or exposing differences.* It is wrong to discriminate[1] for the simple reason that it is wrong to treat people unfairly. In some circumstances, though, it is perfectly acceptable to discriminate[2]. Teachers, for example, are generally expected to give students grades that indicate the extent to which they have mastered course material. Students displaying a high level of mastery on exams and in class discussions might get an A grade, and students with a low level of mastery might get an F. In giving such grades, teachers are discriminating[2] among students, but if the grading is fair, they won't be discriminating[1] against anyone. A teacher who ignores students' mastery of course material and instead grades them solely on the basis of their race or gender, however, *will* be discriminating[1] against students and will therefore be wronging them. And in a perfect world, this teacher would be chastised or even fired for doing so.

A case can be made that discrimination[2] in a classroom isn't just morally permissible, it is morally obligatory. This is because fairness, besides requiring us to *treat like groups alike*, sometimes requires us to *treat different groups differently*. Consequently, unless we discern differences between groups by discriminating[2] among them, we won't treat the groups fairly. In particular, students who neither attend class nor take exams should be given different grades than students who work hard to master course material and subsequently demonstrate this mastery.

My classroom experience suggests that the word "discriminate" is not just emotionally charged; it is "mentally toxic." Hearing it temporarily scrambles students' thought processes. Even after I disambiguated "discrimination" in the manner just described, many of them found it difficult to affirm the claim that "Some forms of classroom discrimination are acceptable." It is an example of how people's heads can, for a time, be hijacked by their hearts and guts.

This same phenomenon occurred in classroom discussions about race. More precisely, students had trouble distinguishing between *racial* and *racist* claims. Racial claims make justifiable assertions about members of a race. Thus, the claim that Black people are more likely to be in prison than white people is a racial claim that is supported by a readily available body of evidence.[3] It is not a *racist* claim, however, because it does not express prejudice against members of a race. Realize that if people refrain from making racial claims for fear of being accused of racism, many important facts will become unspeakable, such as that Black people are more likely to be in prison than white people. This in turn makes it harder to confront racism in the criminal justice system.

For Your Consideration: Answer the following questions

- Is male circumcision morally permissible?
- Is female circumcision morally permissible?
- Is female genital mutilation morally permissible?

When presented with the above questions, most people—in America, at any rate—will respond, without much thought, that male circumcision is morally permissible. It is, after all, widely practiced; indeed, if they are male, they might themselves be circumcised, and if they are a parent, they might have had their male offspring circumcised. The second question about female circumcision, however, will likely require more thought. This is because many people are unfamiliar with the procedure. In their desire to express an opinion, though, they might go through the following thought process: "Surely female circumcision is just the female version of male circumcision, and because male circumcision is permissible, female circumcision is permissible as well. Indeed, wouldn't it be inconsistent—or maybe even sexist?—to think otherwise? So yes, female circumcision is morally permissible." The third question—"Is female genital mutilation morally permissible?"—will be much easier to answer than the second: Acts of mutilation are wrong, so *of course* it is morally impermissible to mutilate female genitals.

Not long ago, these were my answers to the above questions, and I was fairly confident that they were correct. Since then, however, I have done the research that I should have done before forming an opinion, and I was disturbed by what I found. It turned out that the phrases "female circumcision" and "female genital mutilation" refer to the same anatomical procedure, with those who condone the practice giving it the former name and those who oppose the practice giving it the latter. In retrospect, in answering the above questions, I seem to have made not one, but two mental errors. The first was to form beliefs without doing any research. The second was that in the process of forming my beliefs "on the spot," I failed to take into account the emotive power of language.

On doing my belated research, I discovered that regardless of what we call it, the procedure done on girls inflicts pain on them for reasons that are morally difficult to defend. It also dawned on me that similar concerns could be raised with respect to male circumcision.[4]

Rethinking Religion

Before moving on, let's explore parents' motivation for having their infant son circumcised. If asked why they made this choice, they might respond that "It's what people do." By "people" they might mean their ancestors. In particular, a father might have his son circumcised because *his* father had *him* circumcised, because his grandfather had his father circumcised, and so on. Alternatively, the parents might be referring to people in their part of the world. If circumcision was common, they might want their son circumcised so he wouldn't be teased for looking different than the other boys; and if circumcision was rare, they would have decided against it. Parents might instead offer a medical justification for choosing circumcision, including a reduced rate of HIV and urinary tract infections.[5] And not to be forgotten, parents might offer a religious justification. Whereas Sikhs, for example, have religious reasons for not circumcising boys, Jews disagree. Indeed, for Jews, male circumcision is a crucial component of their covenant with God.

We have encountered cases in which people outsource their thinking to a salesperson, a crowd, or an expert. With respect to religion, though, people often outsource their thinking to their ancestors. In particular, they might inherit their religious views from their parents, who inherited them from *their* parents, and so on, back through their family tree. (The most common way to "inherit" a religion is to be raised in it.) In the case of Jews, the chain of inheritance might go back for many generations.[6] Trace it, though, and we will ultimately arrive at someone whose parents weren't Jewish. This person would have discarded his parents' religious views and chosen instead to practice Judaism. Indeed, even if a Jew can trace his Jewish ancestry all the way back to Abraham,[7] he will have arrived at a person who changed his mind about religion: Before his visits from God,[8] Abraham had been a polytheist.

When people adopt their parents' religion, two motivations are often at work. For one thing, it is the intellectual path of least resistance. It requires minimal thought and research on their part, and it won't create problems with their relatives. People might also feel an obligation to stay true to the religion of their ancestors—which is ironic because those ancestors probably wouldn't have held the religion they did unless an earlier ancestor had abandoned the religion of *his or her* ancestors.[9] Shouldn't they therefore countenance people's abandonment of their parents' religion? And more to the point, shouldn't they themselves feel free to abandon their parents' religion?

Later in this book, we will examine a Thinker's decision-making process. If she is making an inconsequential decision, she will probably do so with little thought, but if it is an important decision, she will invest considerable time and effort making it. She might also turn to an expert to make the decision for her—ideally, a fellow Thinker who has a deep understanding of the issues bearing on that decision. She would, however, be appalled by the suggestion that she let a complete stranger make the decision.

If the claims made by many religions are correct, the religion you practice will have a profound impact not just on the quality of your day-to-day life, but far more significantly on the quality of your afterlife: Choose wisely and you will spend an eternity in heaven; choose unwisely and you will spend that eternity in hell. Deciding whether or not to practice a religion—and if you decide to practice one, deciding *which* religion to practice—might therefore be the most important decisions you ever make. They should therefore be made with utmost care.

You won't be doing this, however, if you simply adopt your parents' religion, particularly if they also simply adopted their parents' religion, and so on. Follow the chain back through the generations, and it might lead to an illiterate shepherd who routinely outsourced his thinking to the crowd. Do you really want to give this unknown ancestor so much control over your life—and maybe your afterlife as well?

Take a moment to reflect on your beliefs with respect to religion. You might be an agnostic, in which case you have no beliefs about religion, or an atheist, in which case you believe that God doesn't exist. Alternatively, you might be a theist—maybe a monotheist who believes that only one god exists or a polytheist who believes that many gods exist. And if you are, say, a monotheist, you might believe that the one god wants you to practice one particular religion.

In any of these cases, you owe it to yourself to reexamine your religious beliefs. On doing so, you might end up convinced that your current beliefs are correct or are in need only of minor refinement. You might instead conclude, however, that you don't have good reason to hold the beliefs that you do, or even that those beliefs are mistaken. This might mean changing from an atheist or agnostic to a theist—or conversely. It might mean changing from a monotheist to a polytheist—or conversely. (Reflexively rejecting polytheism, by the way, can be a sign of close-mindedness.)

Alternatively, you might remain a monotheist but change your affiliation from being, say, a Universal Unitarian to being a Jew, Catholic, or Muslim—or conversely. However your reexamination turns out, it will have been an intellectual journey worth taking.

7 | Linguistic Pitfalls

We need language to communicate, but the language we use is flawed. For one thing, it is ambiguous: Words typically have multiple meanings, and as a result, people talk past each other. In such cases, what could and should have been a profitable conversation will become a frustrating experience. And besides one word having multiple meanings, multiple words can have the same meaning. This can create problems when the words in question have different emotional overtones. In some cases, words carry so much emotive baggage that on hearing them, our thought processes temporarily seize up.

But these aren't the only ways in which language is flawed. In our communications, we must take care to avoid what might be described as *linguistic pitfalls*. They may seem innocuous, but they have the power to lead people astray in their attempts to communicate. In this chapter, I will familiarize readers with two of the more hazardous pitfalls so they can not only avoid stumbling into them but maybe help others climb out of them.

Using Words and Mentioning Them

Earlier in these pages, we encountered the question of whether love is just a word, to which I answered, enigmatically, that "it depends." Allow me to explain what it depends on—namely, whether we are *using* the word love or merely *mentioning* it.[1] To better understand this distinction, consider the two sentences displayed below. Both are true, and in each sentence, a word or phrase appears twice. In the first appearance, the word is being *used*, and in the second appearance, it is being *mentioned*:

- Blue is a color, but "blue" is a word.
- The alphabet may have 26 letters, but "the alphabet" has only 11.

In these sentences, we indicate that we are mentioning rather than using a word by enclosing it in quotation marks. There is an easy way to keep track of whether a word or phrase is being used or mentioned: Read the sentence aloud, and when you see left quotation marks, add "the word" or "the phrase," as is appropriate. The first of the above sentences would be read aloud as "Blue is a color *but the word blue* is a word," which is obviously true, and the second of the above sentences would be read aloud as "The alphabet may have 26 letters, but *the phrase* the alphabet has only 11," which is also true. Alternatively, we can "say" the quotation marks: "Blue is a color but, *quote* blue *unquote* is a word."[2] And if people can see us talking, we can employ "air quotes": When we come to the word "blue," we wiggle our index and middle fingers on each hand. Written quotes and air quotes can also be used to indicate skepticism or derision, in which case they are referred to as "scare quotes."

Okay, back to love. For most people, love is a profound emotion, one with the power to transform us as human beings. Other people, though, have a cynical attitude toward love, and on hearing others talk at length about its wonders, one of them might bring the conversation to a halt by dismissing love as being "just a word." On hearing this, a Thinker will—you guessed it—ask for clarification. She might, in particular, ask this cynic to write down his remark. If he writes

> "Love" is just a word.

his claim will be true but trivial and can therefore be ignored: *Every* word is "just a word," including the word "blockhead"! If he instead writes

> Love is just a word.

his claim will be blatantly false because love is an emotion, not a word. So, is love just a word? It depends on whether you are using or mentioning the word "love," and in either case, what you are saying is not worth listening to.

The (spoken) claim that love is just a word is an example of what philosopher Daniel Dennett refers to as a "deepity": It is "a proposition that seems to be profound because it is logically ill-formed. It has (at least) two readings and balances precariously between them. On one reading, it is true but trivial, and on another reading, it is false but would be earth-shattering if true."[3]

The spoken claim that love is just a word is a paradigmatic example of a deepity.

Being exposed to a deepity can boggle a person's mind and might thereby lead him astray in his journey through life. He might, in particular, be drawn into a cult by the deepities uttered by its leader. It is therefore important that we develop our ability to recognize deepities so we can be on the lookout for them. When someone makes a claim that seems simultaneously brilliant and enigmatic—such as that Love is just a word—we should ask for clarification: "Tell me what, exactly, you are trying to say." If he answers by simply repeating the deepity or by unleashing a different deepity, if he refuses to answer the question, or if he belittles us for needing the utterance explained, it is likely that he is spouting nonsense. He might or might not realize that this is what he is doing, but in either case, what he is saying is not worth thinking about and certainly not worth acting on—other than by bidding him adieu.

A Special Kind of Nonsense

Realize that deepities are only one of the linguistic pitfalls we can encounter in our communications with other people. "Category mistakes" are another.

Suppose someone asks whether the sentence "No from if" is true or false. A Thinker will answer that it is neither—that to be true or false, a sentence must be meaningful, and that to be meaningful, a sentence has to be grammatical—which "No from if" isn't. Now suppose this person claims that "Honesty drinks blood."[4] This sentence *is* grammatical. We might therefore be tempted to classify it as false. Do this, however, and we will find ourselves in a logical quagmire. The person making the claim might, after all, respond as follows: "You say that my claim that honesty drinks blood is false. Can I therefore assume that you think honesty *doesn't* drink blood? And by the way, can you tell me what honesty drinks, if not blood?"

According to twentieth-century philosopher Gilbert Ryle, the claim that "Honesty drinks blood" would be neither true nor false but nonsensical, the way the claim that "No from if" is. It is nonsensical for a different reason, though. It lapses into nonsense by committing what Ryle calls a *category mistake*.[5] Honesty simply isn't the sort of thing that is capable of drinking blood—or anything else.

To better understand what Ryle is getting at, consider the following sentence: "The number two is blue." Just to be clear, this sentence, in the way I am using it, isn't asserting that the *numeral 2* is blue, which would be the case if someone used a blue marking pen to write this numeral on a whiteboard. The sentence is instead asserting that the mathematical entity designated by "two" (or "2") is blue. It clearly isn't, though, since mathematical entities don't have colors; nor, for that matter, are they colorless. This is because they aren't in the category of things capable of being colored or colorless. Hats *are* in this category, though, and as a result can be blue, black, or even, in the case of a cellophane hat, colorless. Hats are not, however, in the category of things that can be odd or prime, in the mathematical sense of those words. Thus, if someone said that a hat was prime (in the sense of being evenly divisible only by one and itself), he would be making a category mistake and would therefore be talking nonsense.

Suppose a cult leader tells his followers that even sane people are a bit crazy. He would be speaking the truth because no matter how sane we are, there lurk within us irrational forces that sometimes take control of our life. Suppose, however, that he instead tells his followers—in solemn tones and followed by a pregnant pause—that "Sanity is just another kind of madness."[6] Although this claim sounds profound, it is in fact nonsensical. Although *minds* can be mad, *states of mind* aren't in the category of things capable of being mad. In much the same way, although *you* can be happy, *your happiness* cannot itself be happy—or for that matter, unhappy. The cult leader's claim is therefore nonsensical, and one hopes his listeners realize as much.[7]

In John 14:6 of the New Testament, Jesus tells his followers that "I am the truth." If Jesus had said, "Everything I say is true," it would be a meaningful claim—maybe mistaken, but meaningful. In claiming to *be* the truth, however, Jesus appears to be making a category mistake. *Sentence*s are capable of being true (assuming that they are grammatical). Similarly, *collections of sentences* are capable of being "the truth" (about something). But *beings*, whether they be mortal or divine, simply aren't in the category of things capable of being true or the truth. Although Jesus's claim to be "the truth" sounds profound, it is arguably a nonsensical claim—one, I should add, that might have played a role in some people's conversion to Christianity.

In response to these remarks, a Christian might tell us that it is a mistake to take Jesus literally when he claims to be the truth—that he is instead speaking metaphorically—but this suggestion gives rise to new problems. The first is that just before claiming to be "the truth," Jesus claims to be "the way," and in the very next sentence he announces that "No one comes to the Father except through me." He therefore seems to be saying that he is literally the way to connect with God. Why, then, shouldn't we also take literally his claim to be "the truth"? But suppose that Jesus *is* speaking metaphorically. We are then faced with the task of figuring out his metaphor: In claiming to be "the truth," what, exactly, is he trying to tell us?

A Thinker doesn't object to the use of metaphors as a "step stool" that allows her to grasp something that is currently on a high shelf, out of her reach, but—metaphorically speaking—there had better be something on that shelf! She might, for example, find it useful when her physics teacher, in the process of introducing the concepts of voltage, current, and resistance, employs the metaphor of water flowing through a hose. Similarly, she might find it useful when Nobel laureate Geoffrey Hinton,[8] also known as the Godfather of AI, helps her understand the dangers posed by artificial intelligence by comparing it, in its current form, to a baby tiger: Yes, it is a cute pet, but what about when it grows up?[9] When metaphors are employed by a charismatic individual who is seeking adherents, however, a Thinker will be on guard. She knows how easy it is to come up with seemingly profound metaphors. (Here goes: "I am the echo between silent heartbeats." And if you like that one, I've got more!) She also knows that by doing this, they can lead their adherents down strange and even perilous paths.

Let us end our exploration of category mistakes by taking a moment to consider the meaning of life. When people seek the meaning of life, it is unlikely that they are looking for the meaning of the word "life," and if they are, we can simply direct them to the dictionary. What they are probably looking for is the meaning of *life itself*. If this is the case, though, they are likely making a category mistake. To better understand this point, suppose someone asked you about the meaning of pencils—not the meaning of the word "pencils" but the meaning of *pencils themselves*. Pencils, you would explain, are not the sort of thing that can have meaning. Nevertheless, they can be used to do meaningful things, such as writing haikus or creating grocery lists.

Much the same can be said of life. Like pencils, life itself isn't capable of having meaning, but like pencils, life can be used to do meaningful things. In particular, you can use it to accomplish the life goals you have set for yourself. This, of course, raises the question of which goals are worth accomplishing. Although answering this last question will require deep thought, it is answerable in a way that the meaning-of-life question isn't. It is therefore the question to which you should direct your attention.[10] Bottom line: In seeking the meaning of life, we appear to be making a category mistake. This might be why the "meaning-of-life question," despite having been asked for thousands of years, remains unanswered.

Language is essential if we are to share our ideas with others, maybe to learn from them and maybe to inform or persuade them. But as we have seen, language can be problematic. Words are ambiguous, which can result in us talking past each other. Words can also trigger our emotions, thereby derailing our attempts to engage in evidence-based systematic thinking. And not to be forgotten, there are linguistic pitfalls that can boggle our minds. A Thinker will therefore make it her business to avoid misusing language. She will also be on the lookout for other people's linguistic mistakes. These mistakes, after all, can harm not only those who make them but innocent bystanders—including herself.

PART III

Thinking Our Way Through a Complex World

8 | Understanding Causation

What was the cause of World War I? If you remember your world history, you know the answer: It was Gavrilo Princip's assassination of Archduke Franz Ferdinand of the Austro-Hungarian Empire. Although this may have been the correct answer on the history exam you took, it is clearly incomplete.

To see why I say this, think about guns like the one Princip used. Guns, we are told, kill people, but when you think about it more carefully, you will realize that it isn't guns that kill people, it's the bullets that come out of those guns. And actually, it isn't the bullets that kill people, it's the impact of those bullets with the bodies they hit. No, wait—it's the blood loss that results from the impact that kills them. And we can follow the causal chain in the other direction. It isn't guns that kill people, it is the people who fire those guns that kill people. More precisely, it's the decisions people make that cause them to fire guns, which decisions in turn are affected by the social and political circumstances of the time. Causation, it should be clear, is quite complex.

It is unwise, a Thinker will tell us, to talk about *the* cause of a complex event like World War I; there were instead multiple causal factors—indeed, there was a tapestry of causes— at work. In our research into these factors, we will make a new discovery: Historians disagree over what the significant factors were, as well as the order of the events that led up to an event. Such disagreement is further evidence of how complex our world is.

If we believe that Princip played a key role in the assassination of the archduke, we are confronted with another causal question: What motivated him to do so? It turns out that it is very difficult to fathom a person's motives for acting. Even when someone tells us why he did what he did, we should be skeptical; indeed, in many cases, the *worst* way to find out why someone did something is to ask him. Rather than admitting that he behaved badly, his ego will come up with lies that are so convincing that he himself believes them. In such cases, we would do well to turn to that person's friends and relatives. Yes, they lack direct access to his mind, but their observations of his behavior aren't obstructed by his ego, and as a result they can make a good guess at what motivated him. The world is a causally complex place, and the people who inhabit it are complex beings. A Thinker will keep this in mind in her attempts to understand the world.

Predicting the Future

In some cases, the future is easy to predict: Add baking soda to vinegar, and the mix will fizz. In other cases, because causation is complex, correctly predicting the future is difficult or even impossible. In particular, what seems sure to happen might not happen. I found this out the first time I tried to light logs in a fireplace. I knew that a wad of paper would burn if you held a match under it and that paper was made from logs of wood. I therefore assumed that a log would burn if I held a match under it and was quite surprised when this didn't happen. My prediction failed because I hadn't taken all the relevant causal factors into account. To burn, wood fibers must be raised to a certain temperature, and whereas a match can easily heat a wad of paper to that temperature, it doesn't have the heating power to do so with the surface of a log. The trick to starting a fire in a fireplace: Put the logs over smaller pieces of wood, which in turn are atop wads of paper, and then light the paper.

Even when we know what causal factors are at work, small differences in those factors can make our predictions go awry. This phenomenon is known by scientists as *sensitivity to initial conditions*, and it is known to the world at large as *the butterfly effect*, the idea being that a butterfly in Brazil, by flapping its wings, could conceivably trigger a chain of events that results in a tornado in Texas.[1] If you think this is farfetched, realize that a change involving a few molecules in the DNA of a single COVID-19 virus in China resulted in the deaths of millions of people around the globe.[2] Along similar lines, suppose a speck of dust had caused Princip's gun to jam. As a result, World War I might not have happened. Alternatively, suppose that Hitler had been born with a speech defect that made him reluctant to speak in public. A small thing, to be sure, but it would have dramatically changed the course of history.

Our beliefs about the world usually don't affect it. Our beliefs about how far away the moon is, for example, don't affect that distance. Our beliefs about the value of money, however, do have a real-world impact. In particular, if people stop valuing a currency, it will become worthless. This was the fate of the German mark after World War I, and much more recently, it has been the fate of many cryptocurrencies. Because of this "human factor," predictions can be *self-fulfilling*. Consider, for example, the toilet-paper shortage at the beginning of the COVID-19 pandemic in the spring of 2020. Because people worried that there would be a toilet-paper shortage, they bought it in bulk, resulting in a shortage. Predictions can also be *self-defeating*. Suppose that political pollsters predict, on the basis of the polls they have carefully conducted, that a certain candidate is sure to win an election. In response to this prediction, the candidate's supporters might not bother to vote, and their absence from the polling place might result in the candidate losing the election.

Causal Fallacies

Because causation is so complex, it is easy to go awry in drawing conclusions about what caused what. One such mistake is to engage in what is known as *post-hoc reasoning*: From the mere fact that one event occurred after another, you infer that the first event caused the second. Sometimes this is indeed the case: A peal of thunder was caused by the bolt of lightning that preceded it. Suppose, however, that you had a cold, that on the advice of your grandmother you used a zinc lozenge, and that two days later your cold symptoms had largely abated. You might be tempted to conclude that the lozenge cured your cold, but this inference is fallacious. It is possible, after all, that the cold symptoms would have abated even if you hadn't used the lozenge, in which case using it would have had no causal impact. Someone who routinely feels his way to conclusions might respond to this critique by telling you that he *knows* it was the lozenge that did the trick. If subsequently asked *how* he knows, he might respond,

"I just do"—meaning, one supposes, that he "knows" because his heart and gut tell him so.

Suppose that two phenomena—let us refer to them as P1 and P2—tend to occur together. From this, it does not follow that P1 causes P2. This is because there are four other possibilities:

It could instead be the other way around—that P2 causes P1. By way of illustration, even though there is a correlation between wearing eyeglasses and having bad eyesight, it would be a mistake to infer that people have bad eyesight because they wear eyeglasses; it is the other way around.

It could be that some third factor P3 causes both P1 and P2. Consider, for example, ice cream sales and drowning deaths. Although they are temporally correlated—meaning that over the course of a year they rise and fall together—it is absurd to think that rising ice cream sales cause people to drown, or that a propensity to drown causes people to eat more ice cream. There is instead a third factor, also known as a *confounding factor*, at work—namely, daytime temperature. When the temperature rises, people are more likely both to eat ice cream and to swim, and the increase in swimming can in turn result in an increase in the number of drowning deaths.

There could be "reciprocal causation" between P1 and P2. In such cases, P1 causes P2, which in turn causes P1. For an annoying example of reciprocal causation, put a microphone near a loudspeaker. A causal circle is thereby established and, as a result, the shrill noise known as *feedback* will emanate from the speaker.

The correlation between P1 and P2 could be a mere coincidence. In the early 2000s, Steve Hirdt, executive vice president of the Elias Sports Bureau, discovered that in the presidential election years between 1936 and 2000, there was a strong positive correlation between the outcome of the Washington Redskins' last home football game and the outcome of the subsequent United States presidential election. More precisely, in years when the Redskins won, the party of the incumbent president retained the presidency.[3] This is not just a very strong correlation; it is a *real* correlation—if, at any rate, by "correlation" we mean what statisticians mean. The correlation in question, however, was not the result of causation: How could the outcome of a football game have an ongoing causal impact on the outcome of an election? It was instead a mere coincidence. Think, after all, of how many games and elections one would have to examine to find this correlation. But apparently, Hirdt had nothing better to do with his time. For the record, in 2004 the correlation was broken.

The press is often sloppy in reporting the correlations scientists discover. Suppose, for example, scientists establish that there is a correlation between high sugar consumption and breast cancer. News outlets might subsequently report that "Scientists discover a link between sugar consumption and breast cancer." By doing this, they can attract readers' attention. This is because in the minds of many people, the word "linked" is more suggestive of causation—think about the links in a chain—than the word "correlation." A Thinker will therefore be cautious in her use of the word "linked" and be dubious when she hears others using it.

Doing Experiments to Establish Causation

For event E1 to have caused event E2, E1 must have occurred before E2. This is because "backward causation" is impossible. But as we have seen, from the mere fact that E2 was preceded by E1, it does not follow that it was caused by E1. To prove this, we need to establish that *if E1 hadn't happened, E2 wouldn't have happened.*

If time travel were possible, it would give us a wonderful way to establish causation. We would travel back and prevent E1 from happening, being careful not to change anything else.[4] If E2 subsequently failed to happen, we could conclude that E1 caused it—more precisely, that E1 was a key causal factor. Time travel isn't possible, though, so we must find another way to establish causation.

Experiments are the best way to do this. Think again about the zinc lozenge "cold medicine" previously described. The proper way to test its efficacy is by doing a *controlled experiment*. The first step is to find people who have colds. We randomly divide them into two groups, one of which is designated the *test* (or *experimental*) *group* and the other of which is designated the *control group.* We give the lozenge to those in the test group but not to those in the control group. We also don't let those in the control group take a lozenge on their own. We subsequently track the severity of the colds of the members of the two groups. Suppose that two days into the experiment, those in the test group report that their cold symptoms are much diminished but those in the control group say their symptoms are about the same. This would count as evidence for the causal efficacy of the zinc lozenges.

This experiment can be improved, though. As we have seen, what people believe to be true can affect what *is* true. This human factor can come into play when we do experiments. In the experiment just described, for example, it might not be the zinc lozenge that caused the reduction in cold symptoms. It might instead be the belief, on the part of those in the experimental group, that they had taken something that was alleged to cure colds. This is known as the *placebo effect*: Your physical or mental health is improved by receiving a treatment that has no therapeutic value. You likely experienced a dramatic form of this effect when you were a child. You might have been running around on the playground when you tripped and skinned your knee. You ran to your mother crying, she kissed the knee to make the "boo-boo" get better, and like magic, it did.

It isn't just children who are susceptible to the placebo effect. Researchers have done experiments that demonstrate its power on intelligent adults. One of these experiments involved the treatment of degenerative knee disease. Half of the experimental subjects were given standard arthroscopic surgery. The other half received "sham surgery" in which doctors merely pretended to do the standard procedure: They made an incision in a patient's knee and inserted their arthroscopic instrument, but because its blade had been removed, no internal tissue was cut. After this playacting—which was necessary because the patients were awake during the procedure—they sewed up the incision and subsequently monitored the pain that the patients reported. Their conclusion? The arthroscopic surgery definitely worked, in the sense that the patients subsequently reported less pain and discomfort in the knee that was operated on. To their surprise, though, the sham surgery worked just as well.[5]

These results were widely reported in the press, which in turn triggered pushback from arthroscopic surgeons. In an editorial published in the journal *Arthroscopy*, three of them suggested that any experiment that made use of sham surgery was by its very nature suspect. "What patient in his or her right mind," they asked, would consent to such surgery? And because the patients who volunteered "may not be of entirely sound mind," their subsequent pain self-assessments were not to be trusted.[6] This response brings to mind novelist Upton Sinclair's observation that "It is difficult to get a man to understand something when his salary depends upon his not understanding it."[7] One might conclude that these surgeons' heads had been hijacked not so much by their hearts or guts as by their wallets.

The Gold Standard of Experimentation

Although the experiment involving zinc lozenges is useful, it fails to take account of the human factor. It could be that whatever improvement is reported by those given lozenges is due to the placebo effect. We can eliminate this possibility by supplying both groups with lozenges that look and taste alike but differ in one respect: The lozenges that the test subjects are given contain zinc, while those that the control subjects are given don't. We also need to keep the subjects in the dark about which group they are in and therefore which lozenge they are getting. Do this, and they will presumably experience the placebo effect to the same degree, meaning that any difference in the cold symptoms experienced by the two groups can be attributed to the presence of zinc in the lozenge.

A Thinker will have misgivings about even this improved experiment, though. Because they are only human, the experimenters might long to gain scientific distinction by being the ones who establish the effectiveness of zinc lozenges, and if a lozenge manufacturer is subsidizing their research, they will have a financial incentive as well. As a result, they might unconsciously treat the experimental subjects in the two groups differently, downplaying the cold symptoms reported by those in the test group and exaggerating the symptoms reported by those in the control group. They might, in other words, fall victim to confirmation bias. We can prevent this from happening by keeping not just the subjects in the dark about whether they are getting the zinc lozenge or a placebo but keeping the researchers in the dark as well. This can be accomplished by having a "third party" keep track of which subjects got zinc lozenges and which didn't. Only after the experiment is over and the results for each patient have been recorded will the experimenters find out who got what so they can determine the efficacy of the zinc lozenges.

The experiment I have just described is what is known as a *double-blind controlled experiment.* Such experiments are the gold standard of experimentation, and a Thinker will therefore value them as evidence of causation. (She might do the experiments herself, but it is more likely that she will simply cite experiments that have been reported in scientific journals.) For the record, double-blind controlled experiments have been done regarding the efficacy of zinc lozenges. Some of these experiments suggest that although taking lozenges won't prevent colds, taking them soon after a cold's onset can reduce its duration.[8]

Although doing controlled experiments is a wonderful way to establish causation, there are some experiments that would be morally impermissible for us to perform. Suppose we suspect that exposure to a certain chemical causes people to get cancer. The experiment to confirm this suspicion would be straightforward. We would get a group of people, randomly divide them into a test and a control group, give those in the test group the suspected carcinogen and those in the control group a placebo, and then wait—maybe for years—to see whether cancer develops. It is one thing to do this experiment on rats,[9] but doing it on people would be problematic. They would understandably be reluctant to participate in such an experiment, and if we forced them to do so, we would be violating their human rights.

Under such circumstances, researchers might turn to a so-called *natural experiment*. The first step is to find a group of people who happen to have been exposed to the chemical we are studying. The second is to find a group of people who are very much like those in the first group but have not been exposed to that chemical. We would then compare the cancer rates of the two groups. If the exposed group had a far higher rate of cancer, it would be evidence that the substance was indeed carcinogenic. From a purely scientific point of view, this isn't the ideal way to do things, but it is arguably our best option.

A Thinker's Take on Causation

A Thinker, as we have seen, wants to stay grounded in reality. Doing so, after all, will improve her ability to predict the future which in turn can allow her to shape it. She will therefore take an interest in science and its methods, including the kinds of experiments we've discussed. But she will also investigate particular areas and topics in science, and by doing so gain not just specific knowledge but an appreciation for evidence-based systematic thinking. By studying ecology, she will learn how incredibly complex a causal network can be—how, for example, the disappearance of one seemingly insignificant species from an ecosystem can have an impact on the well-being of the other species. By studying chemistry, she will learn just how long and improbable causal chains can be. By way of illustration, consider the "ozone hole." In 1985, scientists discovered that the ozone over Antarctica was disappearing. Because atmospheric ozone absorbs harmful ultraviolet radiation, its global depletion would have dire consequences for life on land. Scientists therefore set about determining the causal factors responsible for ozone destruction. The primary factor turned out to be the man-made chlorofluorocarbon refrigerants (including Freon) that were released into the atmosphere, mostly in the earth's northern hemisphere. Who would have guessed? Besides studying natural science to better understand how the physical world works, she will study social science to gain insight into how people work. She will, in particular, familiarize herself with psychology, with a special emphasis on its evolutionary and cognitive branches.

By studying her world, she will become aware of just how complex causation is and, as a result, will become skeptical with respect to people's predictions; indeed, the more confident someone is of a prediction, the more skeptical she is likely to be. Such confidence, after all, can be a sign that the person fails to appreciate the world's complexity. She will also become acquainted with the tricks that prognosticators play to make their predictive ability look better than it is. They might lie about having predicted an event or about the substance of a previous prediction. They might also try to fool people by making lots of predictions but subsequently publicizing only those that turn out to be correct, hoping we will forget about the rest.

A Thinker knows that even when a prediction is correct, it might be the result of dumb luck rather than insight. She also knows that the prediction that something is going to happen isn't very useful unless we are also told when it will happen. Timing matters! The prediction that the stock market is going to fall by 50 percent tomorrow, for example, is vastly more useful than the prediction that it is going to fall by 50 percent . . . sometime. Notice, too, that because this last prediction has an unlimited "shelf-life," the person who made it can keep "renewing" it. Along similar lines, religious history is rife with prophets who predicted that the world was about to end. The fact that you are reading these words, however, is proof positive that none of these prophets was correct . . . yet.

Because she recognizes the world's complexity, a Thinker will be guarded in the predictions she makes and might accompany them with caveats. Likewise, whereas a know-it-all will be reluctant to admit being surprised by how events transpire—to do so would be an admission that he doesn't know everything—a Thinker will *expect* to be surprised by what happens in the world around her and will readily admit as much. And finally, if asked about the cause of an event or phenomenon, a Thinker's standard answer will be "It's complicated!" Not only won't there be a single cause, but the various causal factors will be complex.

A "Feeler's" Take on Causation

I will end this chapter by introducing what I shall refer to as *Feelers*, written with an uppercase *F*. Whereas uppercase-*T* Thinkers attempt to optimize their mind by engaging in open-minded critical thinking, Feelers are thought-averse. Rather than relying on their head to draw conclusions, they habitually rely on their heart and gut, and because these organs are incapable of reasoning, Feelers find it difficult to rationally defend the conclusions they have drawn. Consequently, if asked to do so, they might respond not by explaining how and why they reached those conclusions, but by saying, in all sincerity, that "It's how I feel." Alternatively, they might get upset or even angry.

Feelers do exist; indeed, you used to be one. As an infant, you were controlled by your heart and gut. You outgrew this stage, but even now you are capable—perhaps as the result of an overconsumption of alcohol—of lapsing into Feeler mode for a few hours. And should you fall victim to dementia, you might permanently descend into Feeler mode and leave this world the way you entered it, guided solely by your heart and gut.

If you use social media, you routinely encounter Feelers and might be struck by the intensity and incoherence of their rants. Try to engage them in rational discourse, and you will quickly discover that your efforts are futile because such individuals can't be reasoned with. You might also know a Feeler in person. You might, for example, routinely encounter one at extended family gatherings. Strike up a conversation with him,[10] and you might discover that he has outsourced his thinking to an advocacy journalist who daily tells him what he wants to hear with respect to political events and phenomena. This journalist might himself be a Feeler. Alternatively, he might be a very thoughtful individual who has figured out that he can make a good living by providing thought-averse people with simple explanations of complex phenomena and subsequently updating those explanations in light of current events. Clever fellow! Unscrupulous, but undeniably clever.

It is a mistake to assume that the world is neatly divided into Thinkers and Feelers. We should instead imagine an intellectual spectrum, at one end of which would be "pure Thinkers" who habitually think their way to conclusions, and at the other end of which would be "pure Feelers" who habitually feel their way. Most people, however, *will fall somewhere in the middle of this spectrum*, inasmuch as they rely on a mix of reasoning and feeling to reach their conclusions.

Furthermore, although "pure Feelers" do exist—consider your infant self—it is doubtful whether there are any pure Thinkers. Because of how we are wired, our emotions will periodically interfere with our reasoning ability.[11] (And to be clear, this is a good and important part of what makes us human, and we wouldn't want it any other way!) In referring to "Thinkers" in the pages that follow, then, I have in mind not *pure* Thinkers, but those individuals who *routinely make a conscious effort to optimize their mind via open-minded critical thinking*, while at the same time understanding the role that feelings can and sometimes should play in their life. Likewise, the "Feelers" I subsequently talk about include not only the pure Feelers who lack the ability to reason their way to conclusions but those who, although they possess this ability, routinely fail to use it, preferring instead to feel their way. Feeling is, after all, easier than thinking, as well as more emotionally satisfying.

On becoming aware of the Thinker–Feeler distinction, it is tempting to picture yourself and those who agree with you on some topic as being Thinkers and to dismiss those who disagree as being mere Feelers. Realize, though, that your intellectual opponents might be dismissing you in much the same way. If you are indeed a Thinker, you will acknowledge that other Thinkers can disagree with you. Furthermore, even though many or even most of those on the other side of an issue are Feelers, you will acknowledge that Thinkers might lurk among them. One excellent way to establish your *bona fides* as an open-minded critical thinker is by making an effort to find such a person and hear her out: What, exactly, does she believe, and why does she believe it? Such conversations can be simultaneously edifying and humbling. As a result of having one, you might come to realize that your views were mistaken. Rather than being crestfallen about this outcome, though, you might be heartened. It is, after all, a sign that you are making progress toward your goal of mind optimization.

Because she thinks rather than feels her way through life, a Thinker's beliefs will generally differ from those of a Feeler. For one thing, they are more likely to be nuanced, and in particular, she will be less likely to make sweeping generalizations or hold absolutist positions. Furthermore, because they are the result of evidence-based systematic thinking, her beliefs are more likely to be true—more likely, that is, to be grounded in reality—than those of a Feeler. At the same time, though, she is less likely to be emotionally attached to her beliefs, as well as less likely to feel certain that they are true. This means that a Feeler is much more likely than a Thinker to be highly confident of mistaken beliefs, which in turn can lead the Feeler to act on them, perhaps with tragic consequences.

Earlier, I described a Thinker's take on causation. I will end this chapter by contrasting it with that of a Feeler. The latter will be more likely to talk about *the* cause of a complex event. Feelers are also prone to confuse correlation with causation. Why are people getting COVID-19? "It's because of all those cell phone towers they are putting up," a Feeler might insist.[12] More generally, Feelers tend to be anti-science, in the sense that they don't think its findings can be trusted. They have also played a significant role in what has been described as "the death of expertise."[13]

Feelers also have an affinity for conspiracy theories. Such theories, after all, provide them with simple answers to complex questions. Why is the inflation rate rising? "It's because corporations have gotten greedy." The ability to give such answers lets conspiracy theorists feel superior to those who lack their insight into how things "really work." They might also experience the thrill of being in possession of "secret knowledge." Such individuals can be so out of touch with reality that it is impossible to have a meaningful conversation with them, much less convince them that they are mistaken.

You might assume that a Thinker would be uniformly dismissive of conspiracy theories, but this is not the case. She knows, after all, that conspiracies *do* take place. On the Ides of March in 44 BCE, for example, Roman senators conspired to kill Julius Caesar, and during the second half of the twentieth century, American tobacco companies entered into a "conspiracy of silence" to keep people in the dark about the dangers of smoking.[14] Present a Thinker with a conspiracy theory, and she will assess its merits. She will, to begin with, consider the reliability of its source. If the person who proposed the theory seems to have a poor grasp of reality or appears to have personal motives for disseminating the theory—to make money, for example, or to gain an internet audience—she will dismiss his conspiracy theory out of hand. But if the source seems grounded in reality, does not appear to be driven by personal motives, and, significantly, has access to special information, she will ask for supporting evidence. If the evidence provided is unconvincing, she will reject the theory, but if it is cogent, she might come away an ardent supporter of a "conspiracy theory." To behave otherwise, after all, would be close-minded.

9 | Solving Problems in a Complex World

In the course of a day, you typically encounter numerous problems. You might go to the kitchen to make coffee, only to discover that you are out of it. You then go to the garage to start your car so you can drive to work, only to discover that you forgot your keys. You go back inside to get them and return to the car, only to discover that its battery is dead. It's a bad way to start your day, and when you finally get to your workplace, other problems will doubtless await you.

A *problem* can be characterized as a state of affairs that you wish was different. If, for example, you wish you had something that you lack—such as a functioning air conditioner, a late-model car, or a muscular physique—you have a problem. You also have a problem if you wish you lacked something that you have, such as student-loan debt or a disease. Being problematic is therefore a relative notion: What counts as a problem for one person might not count as a problem for another. Also, the more intense your wishes are about how things should be, the more problems you are likely to have. Being finicky comes at a price; adaptability is a blessing.

Most people go through their days encumbered by an assortment of problems. These might include the warning light that appears every time they turn on their car, the pain they experience in their right hip whenever they stand up, and the payment-overdue notice they keep getting from their credit card company. When a new problem arises, they will prioritize it. If a problem is serious and easy to deal with, they will put it at the top of their to-do list. If it is trivial and complicated, though, they might put off dealing with it, and it will thereby take up residence in their unsolved-problem collection, where it will remain until it is either solved or forgotten. The other possibility is that they will learn to live with it, in which case it will, for them, cease to be a problem.

On encountering a problem, a Feeler might complain about how unfair it is for him to have it. He might also expect someone else to solve the problem for him—ideally, for free. If outside help isn't forthcoming, though, the Feeler will have to deal with it on his own, and his problem-solving process will likely be basic. If it is a problem that has arisen before, he will simply deal with it in the usual manner, even though this "patch" might result in the problem arising again in the future. If it is instead a novel problem, he will tend to lean toward obvious solutions that his gut tells him "ought to work."

As we have seen, a Thinker will sometimes outsource her thinking, and in the same way as she might hire a (carefully chosen) expert to do her taxes, she might hire an expert to deal with the problem presented by, say, a broken air conditioner. On confronting a problem that she can't outsource, though, she will be reluctant to trust her gut. She knows, after all, that because causation is complex, very many solutions that "ought to work" not only don't work but exacerbate the problem—or maybe give rise to new problems that are even worse. She will therefore think rather than feel her way to a solution, and she will do so in a systematic manner.

Analyzing a Problem

Before attempting to solve a problem, a Thinker will analyze its structure. This is because she knows that what we regard as *a* problem is often a cluster of related problems, each of which must be dealt with in a different manner. By way of illustration, suppose we return home to find water flooding our bathroom floor. This "flooding problem" is in fact two related problems: Besides the problem of a leaking pipe, there is the problem of the damage being done by the escaped water. How, then, should we proceed? Our first step, a Thinker will tell us, should be to stop the flow of water by turning off the supply to the pipe that is leaking. Our next step should *not* be to fix the leak; it should be to prevent the already-escaped water from doing more damage. Only then should we turn our attention to repairing the leak.

When considering a societal problem, a Thinker will analyze it in a similar manner. Suppose, for example, that she takes an interest in what politicians refer to as *the drug problem*. In the same way as it is a mistake to refer to *the* cause of World War I, it is a mistake to refer to *the* drug problem. This is because there are, in fact, many drug problems; indeed, any problem that arises as a consequence of people using drugs is a drug problem. Yes, opioid addiction is a serious drug problem, but nicotine addiction is arguably an even worse problem because it is responsible for many more deaths. Furthermore, dealing with the problems caused by nicotine addiction will require a different approach than dealing with those caused by opioid addiction. When she hears someone talk about "the drug problem," a Thinker will therefore assume that the person hasn't given the issue much thought and consequently doesn't realize just how complex it is. She will also suspect that he has up his sleeve a pet solution that, although simple and obvious, is unlikely to work.

A Thinker knows that besides having components, a problem can have levels, the way a tree does. Consider, then, the opioid "problem tree." In her analysis of this problem, she might focus her attention up high, on its "twigs and branches," by thinking of ways to reduce the number of overdose deaths. She might, in particular, consider the consequences of making naloxone, marketed under the brand name Narcan, readily available to opioid users. Alternatively, she might focus her attention on the "trunk" of the tree by considering ways to restrict people's access to opioids, maybe by punishing those who transport or sell them, or even those who are in possession of them. And finally, she might focus her attention on the "root" of the opioid problem tree by asking why people become opioid addicts in the first place. On doing this, she will discover that this particular tree has not one root but (at least) two: Whereas some people slip into addiction under the guidance of a medical doctor, others become addicted as a result of using opioids recreationally. Dealing with these two root causes will require different strategies.

Notice that the lower on the tree we deal with the opioid problem, the greater our impact will likely be: If people didn't feel the need to experiment with drugs—if they were satisfied with a sober existence—drug trafficking would plummet, as would overdose deaths. So why, when dealing with a problem, don't we go right to the root? In many cases it is because we think such efforts will be quixotic. Also, considering root causes can force us to think about things we might not want to think about. Why is it, for example, that so many people find a sober existence unsatisfying?

Problem analysis of the sort just described will require a fair amount of thinking, and for this very reason, Feelers tend to skip it. A Thinker, however, knows that the time spent analyzing a problem is time well spent since, as the saying goes, "a problem stated clearly is a problem half solved."[1]

A Systematic Approach to Problem-Solving

On completing her analysis of a problem, a Thinker will embark on her search for the optimal solution. This will typically involve the following steps.

Step one: Come up with a list of possible solutions to the problem. A Thinker will be open-minded in her problem-solving. She will therefore be willing to ask others for possible solutions and will look at solutions that have been developed for similar problems. She will also brainstorm in search of an unconventional or even radically different solution. She knows that if nothing else, the brainstorming process can provide her with important insights into the problem. And finally, she knows that mankind's greatest inventions can be traced back to people who, rather than employing the usual or obvious solution to a problem, doggedly spent the time and effort necessary to think their way to solutions that were clever, elegant, or even brilliant.

Step two: Assess the possible solutions. A Thinker will estimate the cost of implementing each of the solutions on her list.

Suppose, for example, that she is dealing with the leaking pipe described earlier. One solution is to hire a plumber who might charge her $300 to make the repair. Another possible solution, if she is handy, is to fix the leak herself. If she already possesses the necessary material and tools, she will be able to solve the problem "for free"—in monetary terms, at any rate—but she knows that to properly assess a solution, she also needs to take non-monetary costs into account. If she fixes the leak herself, these will include the time spent making the repair, as well as the physical effort required to make it.

A Thinker knows that in some cases, a solution's non-monetary costs will be "human." Suppose, for example, that a general is deciding how to respond to an attack by an opposing army. Besides having costs in terms of money, effort, and time, a battlefield strategy will have a human cost: Soldiers will likely get wounded and die in its implementation. A competent general will take these costs into account.

Besides considering the costs of implementing a possible solution, a Thinker will take into account the consequences of doing so. She knows that because the world is complex, some of these consequences will be difficult to predict. A Thinker also knows that a potential solution to a problem might only partially solve it, might have zero impact on it, and might even exacerbate it. Furthermore, attempts to solve a problem can generate new problems that might be worse than the original problem. We will take a closer look at failed and counterproductive solutions in a moment, in our examination of President Lyndon Johnson's war on poverty and President Richard Nixon's war on drugs.

Besides studying science to improve her understanding of the world, a Thinker will study history. In particular, when confronted with a problem, she will make a point of examining other people's attempts to deal with that and similar problems. What surprises did they encounter? What costs did they overlook, and what consequences did they fail to foresee? She knows that by studying history, she can avoid repeating other people's mistakes. She also knows that the "lesson of history," to the extent that there is one, is that people routinely fail to learn history's many lessons.

Step three: Choose the optimal solution. At this point in her problem-solving process, a Thinker will have a list of possible solutions, an idea of how much it would cost (in an extended sense of the word) to implement each solution, and an idea of the likely consequences of doing so. She will then compare the costs and consequences of the possible solutions to determine which is optimal. There might be a solution that not only solves the problem but does so at a significantly lower cost than the alternatives. For a Thinker, implementing this solution will be a "no-brainer."[2] In many cases, however, there won't be a single stand-out solution. There will instead be multiple plausible solutions, and choosing among them will be tricky.

One thing that makes it difficult to choose among possible solutions is the timing of their costs and benefits. It is tempting to choose solutions that have low up-front costs and deliver benefits immediately. Over the long run, though, implementing such solutions can cost us dearly. Suppose, for example, that someone responds to the burst pipe problem by wrapping it with duct tape. In a matter of minutes, the problem will have been addressed and at a very low cost. In the coming months, though, the tape will likely give way, and the resulting flood might do considerable damage. People who are too savvy to fix a pipe with duct tape might instead get into trouble by deferring maintenance on their car. Yes, they will thereby delay having to spend money, but the cost of repairing their car might be far higher than the cost of having maintained it. A Thinker will realize as much, and she will resist being seduced by short-term thinking.

Another difficulty that arises in comparing costs and benefits is that they often have different metrics. Along these lines, consider again the handy Thinker who is confronted with the leaking pipe. If monetary costs were her only concern, she would do the job herself, but as we have seen, there will also be non-monetary costs, such as the time and effort required to fix it. In choosing a solution, then, she will have to determine the "exchange rate" between the monetary and non-monetary costs. If she is short on time and has a sore back, hiring a plumber would likely be a no-brainer. Suppose, however, that she gets a kick out of making household repairs. By doing so, she not only gets to experience the psychic reward that comes from solving a problem but gets a boost to her self-confidence. As a result, she might make the repair herself even if a plumber offered to do it for free.

To gain a deeper understanding of the role metrics play in problem-solving, let us turn our attention back to the general whose army is under attack. As we have seen, he will take into account the human cost of a battlefield strategy. In particular, he will want to minimize casualties among his soldiers. At the same time, though, he will want to *maximize* casualties among enemy soldiers. From his point of view, after all, such casualties count as a *benefit* of implementing a strategy, not as a *cost*. Furthermore, in choosing a strategy, he will take into account the "exchange rate" between casualties among his soldiers and those among enemy soldiers. Consequently, although he will give serious consideration to a strategy that is likely to inflict a hundred enemy casualties while causing only one casualty among his soldiers, he will reject out of hand a strategy that is likely to cause a hundred casualties among his own soldiers while inflicting only one enemy casualty.[3] Along similar lines, he will reject implementation of a weapon system that, for a price of $1 million, will likely result in only one enemy casualty: Given his values, this would be an ineffective way to spend his budget. (Stated crudely, it wouldn't be a cost-effective way to kill people.) This same general, however, might readily adopt a weapon system that for the same price will likely result in a thousand enemy casualties. In making these choices, of course, he is not only placing a monetary value on human life but is placing a higher value on the lives of his soldiers than on the lives of enemy combatants.[4]

Shifting the example, suppose a hospital is faced with a difficult choice: It can save the life of one patient at a cost of $1 million, or it can use that $1 million to save the lives of a hundred patients. Under these circumstances, it can be argued that because life is precious, the hospital is morally obligated to choose the latter option.[5] A Feeler might find it upsetting that we are confronted by such dilemmas, but alas, we live in a world in which there is a limited amount of money and in which money can't be spent twice. Our goal should therefore be to make the most of what we've got, and the best way to do this is to think rather than feel our way to conclusions. Like it or not, this can require us to attach "price tags" to "priceless" things.

Sometimes a Thinker, when contemplating the possible solutions on her list, will discover that in every case, the cost of implementing a solution outweighs the benefits to be derived from doing so. Stated bluntly, implementing any of the solutions will only make matters worse. Under these circumstances, a Thinker will resolutely do nothing in response to the problem.[6] A Feeler, however, will find it difficult to take this course of (in)action. His gut will insist that he do *something*, and if taking its advice only makes things worse, his heart might provide him with an excuse: "At least I tried!" For a harmful action to be defensible, though, it isn't enough that the actor meant well. If the action wasn't preceded by careful thought, the actor will be guilty of negligence—certainly in the moral realm and maybe in the legal realm as well.

Step four: Implement the chosen solution. After coming up with what looks like the optimal solution to a problem, a Thinker will implement it. If the problem is complex, though, and time and circumstances allow, she might implement it not all at once but in stages. There is, after all, a chance that she has overlooked or underestimated some of the costs of implementing a solution or failed to anticipate some of its consequences.

A Thinker, as we have seen, will be open-minded, and one thing she will be open to is the possibility that her attempt to solve a problem has come up short. For this reason, after dealing with a problem, a Thinker will take a moment to evaluate her efforts. Along these lines, consider again the Thinker who attempted a do-it-yourself repair of the leaking pipe. She might conclude that her repair was a complete success: The pipe is as good as new, and the flooding did no damage. In this case, her self-administered problem-solving grade would be an A. She might instead conclude that her solution was partially successful: Although water is no longer spurting from the pipe, a slight leak remains—a leak she deals with by collecting the dripping water in a bucket that must be emptied daily. In this case, she might give herself a C. She might instead conclude, however, that her efforts *exacerbated* the problem: Before she intervened, water spurted from the pipe; now it positively gushes. This problem-solving effort might earn her a D. Time to call a plumber! And worse still, suppose her attempt to solve the problem gave rise to another, far worse problem: Suppose, for example, that while the Thinker was under the sink using her propane torch to install a new pipe, she accidentally set her house on fire. Time to call the fire department! Her efforts, although well intended, deserve an F.

A Feeler is unlikely to engage in this sort of self-evaluation. One obstacle is the intellectual effort it would require: Too much thinking! Another is his ego, which prevents him from admitting his problem-solving failures to others and, indeed, to himself. If someone criticizes his solution to a problem, he might therefore take offense. He might also resort to counterfactual reasoning in defense of his solution: "It would have worked," he might tell us, "if other people hadn't interfered—so blame them!" Alternatively, he might argue that it would have worked if he had implemented it more aggressively, or that his seemingly failed solution was in fact a (partial) success because the problem would now be much worse if he hadn't implemented it. Counterfactual claims like these, however, are difficult to substantiate.

Because a Thinker consciously looks for her mistakes, she can quickly abandon unsuccessful solutions to a problem. Acknowledgment of her mistakes also reduces the chance that she will repeat them in the future and simultaneously increases the chance that, with the passage of time, her problem-solving skills will improve. Meanwhile, because a Feeler doesn't acknowledge his unsuccessful solutions—or even realize that they have failed—he will not pull the plug on them and might repeat them in the future. Furthermore, he will be likely to overestimate his problem-solving ability and might therefore have a propensity to take on problems that are beyond his level of competence, which can have a negative impact on the lives of those he "helps."

Dealing with Societal Problems

When confronted with a personal problem, we can reason our way to a cost-effective solution and implement it, but when considering a societal problem, we must take an indirect approach. Yes, we can reason our way to what we believe to be a cost-effective solution, but as a mere citizen, we lack the power and resources to implement it. Furthermore, in a democracy our solution will be in competition with those favored by other citizens. And finally, it will be elected officials who ultimately choose which of the possible solutions to implement.

This last step is where things get dodgy. The interests of elected officials don't necessarily align with those of the citizens. One of the primary concerns of these officials is to get reelected; otherwise, they will be out of a job. To get reelected, though, they must convince voters to vote for them. Many of the voters in question, however, will be toward the Feeler end of the intellectual spectrum, and to reach them, a politician would do well to aim his efforts not at their head but at their heart and gut. One very effective way to do this is to bombard them with simple-minded political ads and slogans, and to propose quick and easy solutions to complex problems. Such campaigns are expensive, though, and in raising the necessary funds, politicians find themselves in a bind: Time that could have been spent legislating is instead spent meeting with the lobbyists of special-interest groups. These lobbyists will make campaign contributions in exchange for a promise to support their favored bills. The problem, of course, is that these groups' interests will often be at odds with those of the citizens.

Imagine, if you will, an electorate comprised mostly of people toward the Thinker end of the intellectual spectrum.[7] Under these circumstances, traditional political ads would be a waste of time and money because most voters would ignore them, preferring instead to acquire information that would let them assess candidates' willingness and ability to engage in open-minded critical thinking. Under these circumstances, elections would often be won by candidates who dealt with societal problems in a thoughtful and informed manner, meaning that their solutions would have a good chance of succeeding. Realize, too, that because officeholders wouldn't be in desperate need of campaign funding, they could turn away special-interest lobbyists and focus their attention on citizens' needs. But enough of this daydream! Let's turn our attention back to real-world politicians' attempts to deal with societal problems.

In 1964, President Lyndon Johnson declared war on poverty: What the government should do, he argued, was provide various forms of financial assistance to impoverished citizens. This was the obvious solution to the "poverty problem," and one that many people expected to work. More than half a century and trillions of dollars later, though, the percentage of Americans below the official poverty level is about the same as when the war began.[8] A case can therefore be made that we lost Johnson's "war on poverty," and yet that war is still being waged.

By implementing a government program, we typically bring into existence groups whose well-being depends on its continued operation. In the case of the war on poverty, this includes those who receive poverty relief as well as the bureaucrats and private-sector middlemen[9] who run the programs that provide it. These individuals will back expansion of those programs and fight attempts to curtail them. If a program isn't working, they might argue that it isn't because the program is defective; it is simply underfunded. Although government programs are often difficult to enact, it can be harder still to terminate them. For this reason, when considering the wisdom of enacting a program, a Thinker will take into account how its existence can distort the political landscape.

It's bad enough when a government program fails to solve the problem that engendered it. In some cases, though, implementing a program only makes things worse. President Richard Nixon's war on drugs, declared in 1971, is a case in point. The goal was to dramatically reduce the use of psychoactive drugs by criminalizing their manufacture, sale, and possession. America has clearly lost this war, the evidence being that drug abuse is a vastly bigger problem than it was in Nixon's time. In 1971, for example, there were 3.3 drug-overdose deaths per 100,000 Americans;[10] by 2023, that number was 31.3,[11] an 848 percent increase.

Furthermore, besides failing to solve "the drug problem," the war on drugs gave rise to new problems. Because Nixon's war did not reduce the desire for drugs, it spawned a criminal element willing to satisfy that desire. This in turn triggered gang violence, in which not only gang members but innocent bystanders died.[12] Furthermore, America's prison population swelled; indeed, individuals convicted of drug-related offenses currently constitute nearly half of America's inmates.[13] Americans have also paid a price in terms of their civil liberties. With the war on drugs came "no-knock laws" that allowed police to break into people's homes. The idea was that if police had to knock on a door to gain entry to a residence, someone in possession of drugs could flush the incriminating evidence down the toilet before letting them in. Between 2010 and 2016, eighty-one law-abiding citizens died in these raids.[14]

When dealing with a personal problem, you have an incentive to take account of the cost-effectiveness of potential solutions. You know, after all, that if a solution fails, it is *your* time, money, and effort that are wasted. This is generally not the case, though, when a politician deals with a societal problem. He is likely to underestimate the cost of implementing a solution; he won't, after all, be the one footing the bill. He will instead focus his attention on the potential benefits of implementation.

Earlier in this chapter, we saw how tempting it is to choose solutions that have low up-front costs and deliver benefits immediately. A politician will be subject to these temptations and as a result will be attracted to programs, the benefits of which come quickly—ideally before the next election—and the costs of which come later—ideally, when he has moved on in his political career. In extreme cases of cost shifting, politicians enact measures that benefit current voters at the expense of people who are too young to vote—or for that matter, who haven't even been born! By way of illustration, realize that the payments many elderly citizens receive isn't a return of their contributions to the Social Security program. It isn't even money contributed by other, more affluent citizens. It is instead money "borrowed" from future generations.[15]

10 | Making Decisions in a Complex World

Solve a problem, and under normal circumstances you will have one fewer problem to deal with. This can't be said of making a decision, though. Suppose, for example, that you decide to start your day by going for a walk. The question then arises of what to wear and where to go. There is also the question of what to do while you walk: Should you simply observe the world around you or listen to a podcast? And if you decide to listen to a podcast, which one? The decision to go for a walk will have given rise to many more decisions.

Watch yourself make decisions, and it soon becomes apparent that making them is like trying to slay the mythical Hydra: For each head you chop off—for each decision you make—two new heads appear. As a result, it is likely that over the course of a day, you make thousands of decisions.[1] Most of them are small, though, and making them comes as naturally as taking your next breath.

When you are walking on a smooth sidewalk, you are likely on autopilot. You can focus your attention on other things, and your steps will take care of themselves. Transition to an uneven path with rocks and tree roots, though, and you will have to pay attention to the ground immediately in front of you and make conscious decisions about where, exactly, to step. Encounter a boulder, and you will have to switch from decision-making to problem-solving.² You will consider the various ways in which you can get to the other side of the boulder and choose among the possible solutions to your "boulder problem."

If you drive a car, watch what you do on your next outing. You will find yourself constantly making decisions—about how hard to press on the accelerator, whether and how hard to apply the brakes, whether and how much to turn the steering wheel, and so on. If you are an experienced driver on a route that you have driven many times, these decisions will be made with very little conscious effort. Even though your car isn't literally on autopilot, it is being driven by a person who in some sense is. If you are just learning to drive, though, trips will be mentally taxing because the decisions you make will be conscious decisions.

Suppose that as an experienced driver on a customary route, you are happily "on autopilot," when you see flashing lights ahead. You realize that your route is blocked, and as a result you are confronted with a problem. In solving it, you might resort to the strategies described in the previous chapter: What are the alternate routes you could take, you will ask, and which of them would be optimal?

When you speak, you must make a stream of decisions "on the fly"—which words to use and in what order? You do it effortlessly—unless you are intoxicated or very tired, in which case you might find yourself running aground mid-sentence. When you write sentences instead of speaking them, though, you have more time to choose your words, and as a result, you can carefully ponder word choice and sentence structure. Effortless decision-making thereby transforms into conscious problem-solving. This is one reason writing is more difficult than speaking.

A Systematic Approach to Decision-Making

Because there are so many decisions to make and because many of them must be made quickly, a Thinker's decision-making process will generally be more rudimentary than her problem-solving process. She might, in particular, engage in basic pros-and-cons reasoning. Suppose, for example, that she is deciding whether to go for a walk at sunrise. Among the pros: She will benefit from the exercise and fresh air. Among the cons: She won't be able to sleep in and will have to get dressed earlier than would otherwise be the case. She will then weigh the pros against the cons, and if the pros prevail, she will take the walk.

A Thinker might add a dimension to her pros-and-cons assessment by considering the contingencies that affect the consequences of making a certain decision. Suppose, for example, that she has decided to take a long walk. This decision will give rise to new decisions, such as whether to bring food and water, and whether to bring an umbrella. In making this last decision, the relevant contingency is the weather. If it is going to rain, she will benefit from having brought an umbrella, but if rain is unlikely, the umbrella will be an encumbrance. If, however, it is going to be both rainy and windy, it would be foolish to bring an umbrella; what she instead needs is a raincoat. She will also take into account the likelihood of each contingency. The higher the probability of rain, for example, the more reason there is to bring an umbrella—or maybe a raincoat. In making a decision, a Thinker will also take into account the impact that choosing a particular option will have on her future options; indeed, if a decision is significant, she will resemble a chess player who, on deciding which move to make next, will ponder its impact on subsequent moves.

People change with the passage of time. A seventy-year-old woman, for example, will have markedly different interests and values than she did at age seventeen, which in turn were different than those she had at age seven. If she knew what she was going to want in the future, she could take this into account in making important decisions. The problem is that she doesn't know. It is an awkward situation to be in. There is an offsetting factor, though. The decisions we make can have an impact on our self-identity, which in turn will have an impact on our values.[3] On deciding to become parents, for example, a couple's values are likely to shift dramatically. They might, in particular, take pride in their parenting ability, and this pride will make the challenges of parenthood more tolerable.

Suppose a Thinker is faced with a major decision. Suppose, for example, that her employer has offered her an early-retirement buyout. In some cases, she will have little trouble deciding what to do. If she hates her job, for example, the buyout might be a godsend, and if she loves it, saying no to the buyout might be a no-brainer. If she is in neither of these categories, though, the choice won't be obvious. Under these circumstances, she will still engage in pros-and-cons reasoning, but in a more sophisticated manner.

The first step will be to consider a number of relevant factors. How would taking the buyout affect her quality of life? She has a good idea of what continuing to work would be like, but what if she retired? Would she be bored, or would she find fulfilling alternatives to working? She will also consider practical issues: If she took the buyout, what would her health-insurance situation be? And not to be forgotten, she will investigate how taking early retirement will affect her finances. Doing this might involve creating one or more spreadsheets. It might also involve consulting (carefully chosen) experts. On completing her research, she might construct a pros-and-cons list, to make sure she hasn't left something important out. She will then weigh the pros against the cons and make the optimal choice.

Feeling Your Way to a Decision

Whereas a Thinker makes decisions with her head, a Feeler will typically rely on his heart and gut. Besides requiring less mental effort, this manner of making decisions takes less time. Consequently, a Feeler might, in a matter of seconds, make a decision that a Thinker might take hours, days, or even weeks to make. Feelers are also capable, though, of putting off decision-making. Suppose, for example, that someone offers an unemployed Feeler a job and gives him a week to reply. He might dillydally for so long that the deadline passes without a decision having been made, at which point he will have "chosen" to remain unemployed. Later in this chapter, we will see how a Thinker's decision-making process can reduce her susceptibility to such procrastination.

After making his decision, a Feeler might not have much to say in defense of it: "To me, it just felt like the right thing to do." By way of contrast, a Thinker will be able to describe the factors she took into account as well as their relative importance. Thus, although both the Feeler and the Thinker will have made a decision, only the Thinker will have made a *considered* decision. As we have seen, her goal in forming beliefs is to optimize her mind—to fill it, to the extent possible, with true and useful beliefs. Her goal in decision-making will be to optimize her *life*—to have the best life she can, given her circumstances and values.

Before moving on, let me add that the pros-and-cons decision-making procedure is susceptible to manipulation. Someone constructing a list of pros and cons might, for example, "adjust" the list he is evaluating by adding pros and removing cons so the evaluation will conform to the wishes of his heart and gut. Alternatively, someone might wait until *after* he has made a decision to create a pros-and-cons list. In doing so, he isn't using the list as a tool for rational decision-making; he is instead using it to rationalize a decision that his heart and gut have already made.

On hearing about the effort a Thinker puts into making decisions, a Feeler might respond that it must be awful to be constantly worrying about the future and might offer some advice: Instead of obsessing about her future path through life, the Thinker should follow his example and "live for today." A Thinker might respond to such comments by pointing out that there is a difference between being anxious and being thoughtful: You can be anxious without being thoughtful, and you can be thoughtful without being anxious. Furthermore, the more thoughtful you are, the less anxiety you are likely to experience in the future.[4] This is because you will have anticipated many of the problems that can arise, taken steps to prevent them, and devised strategies for ameliorating the impact of those that cannot be prevented. As a result, rather than feeling anxious about the future, you can proceed with a degree of confidence.

Do you want to avoid needless anxiety? Then endeavor to make decisions with your head rather than with your gut.[5] Because your gut can't think, your gut-level decisions are likely to be suboptimal, and as a result, you will routinely find yourself in difficult circumstances—at which point your gut might respond by tying itself into a knot of anxiety. Singularly unhelpful!

If a Thinker knew she was going to die at midnight, she would make a point of "living for today." Chances are, however, that rather than dying at midnight, she will be around for a long, long time. She knows that by spending part of today thinking ahead, she lays the groundwork for an enjoyable future existence. Yes, her anticipatory actions require thought and effort, but she will construe such actions not so much as a sacrifice but as a gift from her present self to her future self. Realize that if you are reading these words, it is because your childhood self learned how to read. If time travel is ever perfected and you thereby gain the ability to visit your younger self, be sure to thank him or her for having spent the time and effort necessary to acquire this skill. And as long as you are in that part of the space–time continuum, why not also thank those who taught you how to read?

We have seen how listening to your heart and gut can give rise to inconsistent beliefs. It can also give rise to inconsistent behavior. More precisely, it can cause you to act at cross-purposes with yourself, with the decision you make today reversing a decision you made yesterday. As a result, a Feeler's journey through life can resemble an aimless ramble. By thinking rather than feeling her way to decisions, a Thinker will reduce this sort of backtracking. This increases the chance that she will attain the things she values and thereby increases the chance that she will have a life that, given those values, is worth living.

Was It the Right Decision?

Most people, when assessing a decision they have made, focus their attention on its outcome: If the decision had a good outcome, it was a good decision, and if it had a bad outcome, it was a bad decision, period. A Thinker, however, will distinguish between how *beneficial* a decision turns out to be and how *prudent* it was to have made it. A decision is prudent if she carefully and thoughtfully considers the pros and cons of making it. (In assessing a decision, we need to take into account the circumstances under which it was made: A decision that had to be made in twelve seconds with limited access to information should be judged by a different standard than a decision that was made over the course of twelve days and with ready access to information.) She can therefore determine the prudence of a decision immediately after making it: She need only reflect on the process by which it was made. By way of contrast, to determine whether a decision is beneficial, she will have to wait for the future to unfold.

To better appreciate the distinction between prudent and beneficial decisions, suppose that when a pregnant woman starts experiencing frequent and intense contractions, her husband rushes her to the hospital. It is the prudent thing for him to do, don't you think? But suppose that on the way there, a drunk driver slams into their car, killing both the woman and her unborn child. Judged by its consequences, the decision to go to the hospital won't have been beneficial; to the contrary, it will be a tragic decision to have made. Prudent decisions therefore needn't be beneficial. Conversely, decisions can be beneficial without being prudent. Suppose, for example, that a man bets his $100,000 life savings on the number seventeen in roulette. It is an imprudent thing to do because there is a 97.4 percent chance that he will go broke.[6] In the unlikely event that the number seventeen does come up, though, his net worth will rise to $3,600,000, a very nice outcome. In this case, the decision to gamble, though not prudent, will turn out to have been quite beneficial.

Judging decisions by their consequences rather than their prudence raises other issues. There is, to begin with, the *time frame problem*. With the passage of time, the consequences of a decision can switch from good to bad and back again, raising the question of when, exactly, we are to make our "official assessment" of its consequences. To better understand this point, consider the parable of the farmer with a runaway horse.[7] On hearing about the horse, his neighbors came to console him: "That's too bad," they said. The farmer's reply: "Maybe." The horse soon returned, accompanied by seven wild horses. "That's great!" his neighbors exclaimed. The farmer's reply: "Maybe." The following day, his son tried to ride one of the wild horses to tame it but was thrown and broke his leg. "That's too bad," his neighbors told him. "Maybe," said the farmer. The day after that, military officers came to the village looking for conscripts, but because the son's leg was broken, they rejected him. "Isn't that wonderful!" his neighbors exclaimed. You can doubtless guess the farmer's reply. So, was a decision we made yesterday—or last month or last year—beneficial? Maybe, but we would do well to revisit it in the future. Much the same, I should add, can be said with respect to problem-solving. With the passage of time, a solution that initially looked brilliant can turn out to have been a huge mistake.

In the business world, people's decisions are often judged by their consequences rather than by the process used to make them, but this seems unfair: Although we have it in our power to make decisions thoughtfully, we cannot control what our uncertain world does thereafter. Consequently, to blame us, with perfect hindsight, for how things turn out is like blaming the previously described husband for taking his wife to the hospital. And besides being unfair, this sort of scapegoating can be counterproductive. In the business world, when someone who, despite having made a decision thoughtfully and carefully, is punished for its consequences, other employees learn an important lesson: They will avoid making decisions, and if forced to do so, will do their best to spread the responsibility for those decisions. They will also focus on the short-term consequences of their decisions because these are easier to predict, even though their company might benefit from them taking a longer-term perspective.

If we had a complete understanding of our world, it would make sense to focus our time and effort on making decisions that we knew would have beneficial consequences. Because we lack such an understanding, though, our goal should be to invest the time and effort necessary to make prudent decisions. Such decisions, after all, are more likely to have beneficial consequences than unconsidered decisions, meaning that in the long run, making prudent decisions maximizes our chance of flourishing in the days that lie ahead. Bottom line: With respect to decision-making, we should focus on *process* rather than *outcome*.

We have seen that a Feeler's reliance on his gut instincts enables him to make decisions on the spot. Nevertheless, that same Feeler might procrastinate when called upon to make an important decision. This hesitance is partly a consequence of a fear that he will live to regret making a "bad decision"—a decision, in other words, with undesirable consequences. A Thinker, however, will be relatively free of such fears. If a thoughtfully made decision has bad consequences, she won't beat herself up. She will know, after all, that despite its consequences, it was a prudent decision to have made.

Decision-Making Shortcuts

Because money is precious, a Thinker will budget her income: She will, in particular, take care not to waste it. She will likewise budget her time. And because thinking requires both time and energy, she will budget her thought; she will, in other words, develop strategies for thinking more effectively. Some of these strategies will come into play in her decision-making. Faced with a trivial choice, for example, she might make a snap decision. She might also give herself decision-making deadlines: Besides preventing procrastination, such deadlines give her an incentive to make decisions in an efficient manner. And finally, she will employ decision-making shortcuts, two of which we will now explore.

Adopt RULES for living. As we go about our daily business, we routinely find ourselves in situations that require us to make decisions. When there is reason to think that a situation is likely to recur, we might lighten our future decision-making burden by adopting a "rule for living." By way of illustration, suppose a Thinker is offered an extended warranty for a consumer product. If it is the first time this has happened, she might take a few minutes to figure out whether such warranties are worth buying. On determining that for most consumers in most situations they aren't, she might not only decline the warranty but adopt a rule for living: "Decline extended warranties on consumer products." After that, when offered an extended warranty, she won't need to give the matter any thought. She will simply decline the offer.

You have likely adopted many rules for living, but because they are so ingrained, you are oblivious to your reliance on them. At present, for example, my e-mails customarily start with, "Hi, X," (with a "vocative comma" between the greeting and the name) where X is the first name of the person who wrote to me. It is an example of a conscious decision, made in the early days of e-mail, metamorphosing into a decision-making shortcut. I also have rules about how to load a dishwasher, how to make coffee, and when to use a semicolon. By adopting such rules, we can lighten our decision-making burden. On finding ourselves in a certain situation, we don't need to decide what to do; we've already decided. Follow a rule for living for awhile, and it will morph into a habit.

Such rules must be used with caution. There is, after all, a chance that a rule for living is misguided. This might be because the original decision—the one that gave rise to the rule—overlooked important considerations. And even if the original decision was prudent, the world might subsequently have changed in a way that renders it obsolete. A Thinker will therefore be open to revisiting her rules for living.

Adopt ROLES for living. Besides adopting rules for living, a Thinker will engage in role-based decision-making. To do this, you decide what kind of person you are and then, when called upon to make a decision, you act the way that sort of person would act. By way of clarification, suppose you see a wallet fall out of a woman's purse. You then have a decision to make: You can tell her what has happened, or you can wait till she walks away, grab the wallet, and take its contents. For some people, this will be a difficult decision, with lots of second-guessing. For most people, though, the decision will be easy: Because they have decided to play the role of honest person, they will simply tell the woman. This, of course, is only one of many roles that you can adopt, including the role of being a kind, brave, or generous person. And not to be forgotten, you can choose to play the role of being a Thinker.

Instead of acting the way a certain sort of person would, you can decide to act the way a particular individual would. For example, when called on to make a decision, a practicing Christian might ask, "What would Jesus do?" Although I don't practice any religion, I am a practicing Stoic.[8] As a result, I often find myself asking not what Jesus would do under certain circumstances, but what Marcus Aurelius would do. When lying comfortably in bed in the morning, for example, I might ask myself what Marcus would do. Fortunately, he addressed this very question in his *Meditations*: "At dawn, when you have trouble getting out of bed, tell yourself: 'I have to go to work—as a human being. What do I have to complain of, if I'm going to do what I was born for—the things I was brought into the world to do? Or is *this* what I was created for? To huddle under the blankets and stay warm?'"[9] It is advice that has pried me out of bed on many a cold January morning. Before moving on, I should add that the Stoic philosopher Seneca, whom I also use as a role model, himself advocated the use of role models: "Choose someone whose way of life as well as words . . . have won your approval. Be always pointing him out to yourself either as your guardian or as your model."[10]

While I can't guarantee that the decision-making strategies provided in this chapter will ensure that your decisions have happy outcomes, using these strategies will substantially increase the chance that they do, and in this uncertain world, that is as much as you can hope for.

PART IV

Cognitive Biases

11 | Confirmation Bias

Trace your family tree back—way back—and you will arrive at creatures who had emotions but limited ability to reason. Move down the tree—toward yourself—and you will encounter creatures who, because they had acquired a prefrontal cortex, had modest reasoning ability. Realize that this cortex didn't *replace* the limbic system responsible for their emotions; it simply took up residence nearby. As a result, although they could think, their reasoning process could be influenced and even sidetracked by their emotions. They were therefore mental hybrids, as are you, their descendant.

Being a hybrid isn't easy. It means that on a daily basis, you must deal with skirmishes between your head, which tries to reason its way through life, and your heart and gut, which try to feel their way. And to make matters worse, your reasoning ability is defective. Don't take this assertion personally, though. The same can be said of every human being. It is a consequence of how we evolved.

Ten million years ago, your primate ancestors had sufficient brainpower to engage in associative thinking. If they got sick eating a certain plant, they might associate it with unpleasant feelings and would therefore avoid it in the future. With added brainpower, this associative thinking became more complex: If they saw someone else get sick after eating a plant, they would avoid eating it. They would also generalize: On getting bitten by a snake, they might subsequently avoid not only that kind of snake but anything that slithered, as well as the area where the snake bite took place. It was a crude form of thinking, and as a result, many of the conclusions they drew were mistaken. Given their circumstances, though, crude thinking was better than no thinking at all. It was good enough to improve their chance of surviving and reproducing, which from an evolutionary perspective is what matters.

A tendency to overgeneralize turns out to be only one of many mental shortcuts that are evolutionarily wired into us. Psychologists refer to these shortcuts as *cognitive biases*, and led by Daniel Kahneman and Amos Tversky, they have discovered and studied dozens of them, including the following:

- We commit the *anecdotal fallacy* when we ignore statistical evidence about a phenomenon in favor of a story about a single case.
- We commit the *gambler fallacy* when we think that a coin coming up heads five times in a row makes it more likely that it will come up tails on the next toss.
- We experience the *backfire effect* when we respond to a challenge to one of our beliefs by clinging to it even more tightly.
- We experience *zero-sum bias* when we think that for someone to gain, someone else must lose.
- We commit the *planning fallacy* when we underestimate the amount of time it will take us to do something.

- We experience the *rhyme-as-reason effect* when hearing a claim stated in the form of a rhyme increases our confidence that it is true. Seriously!

It is not possible, in these pages, to explore all the cognitive biases.[1] We will instead focus our attention on two that are of particular interest because of the harm they have done to humanity. In this chapter, we will explore our tendency to seek evidence that confirms[2] our current beliefs, and in the next chapter we will explore our tendency to overestimate our understanding of a subject.

What Is Confirmation Bias?

Suppose that as an election draws near, you find yourself leaning toward Candidate A. It isn't that you *decided* to lean; you simply discovered that you *were* leaning. What might be called a *belief seed* has somehow drifted into your mind, perhaps as a result of having a conversation, hearing a political slogan, or seeing a bumper sticker. Although this seed has somehow attached itself to you, your mind isn't particularly attached to it. The seed might therefore be forgotten or dislodged by another belief seed. Nurtured by confirmation bias, though, it might take root and transform into an unshakable belief. Here is one way this can happen.

On discovering that you are leaning toward Candidate A, you might make an effort to learn more about her. After sampling different news sources, you might keep returning to one that praises her and avoid those that criticize her or, even worse, that say good things about Candidate B, her rival. You might even start avoiding people who disparage Candidate A. You might also become biased in your interpretation of events. On encountering a video showing Candidate B using what seems to be an ethnic slur, you might unhesitatingly accept its authenticity and gleefully share it online. On encountering a video showing Candidate A making a similar remark, though, you might dismiss it as being an obvious fake; alternatively, you might accept its authenticity but assume that the remark was taken out of context. Engage in this sort of behavior, and there is an excellent chance that you have unwittingly fallen victim to confirmation bias.

Confirmation bias isn't choosy. It is indifferent to whether a belief seed is correct or mistaken. It is also indifferent to its source. It will nurture whatever belief seeds are present in your mind, looking for evidence that supports them and ignoring, distorting, or dismissing evidence that challenges them. You might assume that by doing extensive research, you can circumvent the acquisition of mistaken beliefs, but if your research is distorted by confirmation bias, it can instead increase your confidence in the truth of what is in fact a mistaken belief.

Once you know what to look for, you will realize the pervasiveness of confirmation bias. After diagnosing an illness in a patient, for example, a doctor might look for evidence that his diagnosis is correct and ignore evidence to the contrary, which can have disastrous consequences for the patient. After identifying someone as their prime suspect, police might redouble their effort to look for evidence that he is guilty but stop looking for exonerating evidence and dismiss as irrelevant any that they stumble across. Innocent people have gone to jail as a result. In the business world, a CEO might surround herself with sycophants who tell her what she wants to hear. This practice, however, puts her out of touch with economic reality, which can hurt her company. Leaders of countries are likewise prone to surround themselves with sycophantic advisors, which can have disastrous consequences for the citizens of their country, as well as for the leaders themselves.

Confirmation bias has played a crucial role in the history of religion. Many religions are founded by individuals who believe that God has chosen them as his agent on Earth. Having formed this belief, though, a prophet becomes susceptible to confirmation bias. He might, for example, start assuming that his dreams are messages from God; indeed, he might start referring to them as *revelations* or *visions*. His followers might likewise succumb to confirmation bias. When he describes one of his dreams, they won't respond in an understandably skeptical manner: "That's just a crazy dream. I have them all the time!" They will instead take the dream seriously and accept it as evidence of his special relationship with God. Meanwhile, they might be quick to reject evidence that their prophet is delusional or an outright fraud. They will also reject the claims made by rival prophets, even though these claims are supported by similar dreams.

Because they are smart and well-educated, we might assume that scientists would be immune to confirmation bias, but this is hardly the case.[3] Scientists who do experiments to test a hypothesis that they favor might bend over backwards to come up with publishable evidence in support of it,[4] and when they come across evidence to the contrary, they might invest considerable intellectual effort trying to explain it away. The work of scientists—and in particular, social scientists—can also be influenced by their religious, political, and social beliefs. It would be bad enough if scientists who fell victim to confirmation bias wasted their own time and maybe their career. Their misguided efforts, however, can delay the progress of science by sending other researchers down blind alleys.

Avoiding Confirmation Bias

A Feeler will likely be unaware of confirmation bias, and if we explain it to him, he might be unconcerned by the role it plays in his life. Indeed, from his perspective, rather than being an intellectual hazard, confirmation bias might count as a useful psychological phenomenon because it allows him to feel his way toward an agreeable conclusion with little, if any, thought. Not only that, but on arriving at that conclusion, confirmation bias relieves him of the burden of having to reconsider it in light of new evidence. He can instead simply dismiss that evidence.

A Thinker, however, will be deeply troubled by the way confirmation bias can distort people's thinking—including her own. She knows that such bias can lead her not just to adopt mistaken beliefs but to become quite confident that they are correct. She also knows that once these beliefs have been adopted, confirmation bias can cause her to ignore, dismiss, or explain away evidence that they are mistaken. As a result, her mind can end up not just closed but hermetically sealed with respect to a subject. A Thinker realizes that unless she makes a conscious effort to avoid confirmation bias, this will be her fate.

A Thinker, as we have seen, will be quite selective in gathering the information and evidence necessary to arrive at an informed conclusion. She will favor some sources—scientific journals, for example—while avoiding other sources, such as internet conspiracy sites or social media posts. She will likewise be discriminating in her response to evidence that challenges the conclusions she has drawn. If a flat-earther presents her with what he claims are satellite images showing the earth to be flat, she might dismiss his "evidence" without even giving it a glance. In behaving this way, though, she will look suspiciously like someone in the grip of confirmation bias, but this won't necessarily be the case.

In forming a new belief, a Thinker will do her research with a mind that is open but not too open. Rather than picking information sources in a random manner, she will judge how reliable they are and choose accordingly. More precisely, she will judge the expertise of the people responsible for the information in question, and she will assess the process they used to acquire that information. As a result of this selectivity, the Thinker will ignore some sources altogether, but it is not because what they say is at odds with her beliefs. It is instead because she has reason to think that they either don't base their conclusions on reliable evidence or that the process they use to draw those conclusions is logically or psychologically suspect. She will also ignore sites run by individuals whose objective, rather than propagating what they believe to be the truth, is to profit financially by propagating lies. Listening to what they say would therefore be a waste of time and brainpower. Consequently, her selectivity won't be a symptom of confirmation bias. It will instead be evidence that she spends her "thought budget" wisely.

Although a Thinker will ignore or quickly dismiss the claims made by many Feelers, she will take quite seriously the claims made by her fellow Thinkers, even when those claims are at odds with her beliefs. She engages in this sort of intellectual discrimination because she knows that whereas Thinkers will be willing and able to describe the evidence and inferences that led to their conclusions, Feelers won't.

If a Feeler resents being brushed off in this manner, a remedy is at hand: He need only make a point of trying to think rather than feel his way to conclusions. He might subsequently discover that in much the same way as exercising can strengthen your muscles, thinking can strengthen your mind, and that in much the same way as it feels good to be physically fit, it feels good to be mentally fit. As a result, he will start sliding toward the Thinker end of the intellectual spectrum and might eventually join the Thinker ranks. Such things do happen!

Ideologies Reconsidered

I will end this chapter by exploring ideologies and the role they play in our thinking. There are hundreds of ideologies, including liberalism, environmentalism, feminism, social Darwinism, and Marxism, which in turn have variants. Besides Marxism, for example, there is Maoism, Marxism-Leninism, Structural Marxism, and Neo-Marxism. Ideologies have played an important role in human history. Although we can argue about whether the appearance of a particular ideology changed things for the better or for the worse, it is clear that ideologies have had a substantial impact on people's lives—and in the case of environmentalism, on the planet they inhabit.

By familiarizing ourselves with ideologies, we gain important insights. Study Marxism, and we become aware of the predicament of wage earners, how the profits of a business are distributed, and the motives of owners. Study capitalism, and we become aware of the risks taken by those who start businesses as well as the incentives that affect their business decisions. Study feminism, and we become aware not only of sexist behavior but of the systemic sexism that is embedded in the procedures, routines, and cultures of many organizations. Besides making us aware of what is going on around us, ideologies provide an explanation of why things are the way they are. Ask a feminist why sexism exists, and she will likely introduce the concept of a patriarchy. Along similar lines, ask a Marxist why the economy is experiencing an economic downturn, and he will be ready with a thoughtful explanation; ask a capitalist instead, and he will be ready with an explanation that, though substantially different, is also thoughtful.

A Thinker will regard ideologies as intellectual tools that are simultaneously useful and dangerous. One of her primary goals, as we have seen, is to keep an open mind. In particular, she knows that because the world is a complex place, it is important for us to look at it from multiple perspectives. Ideologies do a wonderful job of providing those perspectives. At the same time, though, she will be concerned about ideologies' ability to capture peoples' minds. Fall under the spell of an ideology, and she will be tempted to see some aspect of the world exclusively through the lens that it provides, and as a result she will become less open-minded.

To better understand this phenomenon, think about *masculinism* (also known as *masculism*). Whereas feminism is concerned with sexual discrimination against women, masculinism is concerned with sexual discrimination against men. Study feminist ideology, and you will be exposed to many examples of sexual discrimination against women. It is unlikely, however, that you will be exposed to examples of sexual discrimination against men, and if you are, their significance will likely be downplayed. It is therefore easy to come away thinking that sexual discrimination against men isn't possible, or that although it is possible it is rare and that when it does occur it isn't a big deal. As a result, on hearing about masculinism, someone imbued with feminist ideology might snort in derision: "Men aren't the *targets of* discrimination; they're the ones *doing* the discriminating!"

On being dismissed in this manner, a masculinist—who needn't, by the way, be male[5]—might offer statistics like the following. In the United States, men typically live six years fewer than women. They are much more likely than women to commit suicide, as well as being ten times more likely to be incarcerated. Men are also significantly less likely to graduate from high school; if they graduate, are significantly less likely to go to college; and if they go, are significantly less likely to acquire a degree. A reflexive feminist might simply dismiss these statistics as irrelevant, but a more thoughtful feminist will try to account for them. Why is it, for example, that women are more likely than men to graduate from high school and more likely to obtain a college degree? It might be because men are less studious than women. This response, however, doesn't get to the bottom of things. Could it be that men are less studious because their teachers—often women—treat them differently or have lower expectations for them? And could it be that women are more likely to get college degrees because those degrees have greater financial value for them than for men?[6] This last phenomenon, a masculinist might argue, is an unintended consequence of affirmative action on behalf of women.

I will not attempt to settle the feminism–masculinism debate in these pages. I raise it only to illustrate the manner in which ideologies can take us captive by lulling us into a deep state of confirmation bias with respect to a subject. As a result, we find ourselves dismissing evidence that undermines our views. More strikingly, we might find ourselves dismissing evidence which, if "reversed," we would readily offer in support of our views. Suppose, for example, that it was *women* who lived six years fewer than men and suppose that *women* were ten times as likely to be incarcerated as men. Many feminists would put this evidence front and center in their argument that women are discriminated against. This disparate treatment of evidence suggests that they have been taken captive by their feminist ideology. Rather than being a tool that gives them an important perspective on the world, it has become a telescope, the lens of which is tinted and maybe distorted as well.

Many of those who take part in the feminism–masculinism debate proceed on the assumption that either women are discriminated against or men are, but not both. Realize, though, that if by "discriminate" we mean *unfairly treat a person or group of people differently from other people or groups*,[7] it is entirely possible for *both* women *and* men to be the targets of discrimination. That said, if there were reason to think that discrimination against women did substantially more harm than discrimination against men, dealing with the former kind of discrimination might be our priority, but from this it does not follow that we should simply ignore the latter form of discrimination.

A Thinker won't be anti-ideology; indeed, she will make a point of exposing herself to multiple ideologies. The perspectives they provide, after all, can help her see things to which she would otherwise be oblivious. At the same time, however, she will guard against being taken captive by the ideologies she explores.

12 | What Do You Know?

In the words of eighteenth-century poet Alexander Pope, "A little learning is a dangerous thing."[1] After learning a little about a subject, we tend to think we know a lot about it, far more than we in fact do. Late in the twentieth century, psychologists David Dunning and Justin Kruger made Pope's insight the focus of a proper scientific study. They found that if you take someone who is utterly ignorant of a subject and provide him with a bit of information, he will quickly conclude that he knows a lot about the subject—indeed, almost everything that is worth knowing.

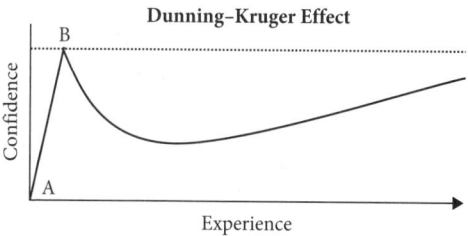

This phenomenon, which subsequently became known as the *Dunning–Kruger effect*, is illustrated in this graph. The point (A) in the lower left-hand corner represents someone who is new to a subject. He knows nothing about it and will therefore have zero confidence in his understanding of it. Give him a little information, though, and his confidence will skyrocket. Lots of people are happy to remain atop this pinnacle (B) in the curve. It feels great, after all, to think that you have pretty much mastered a subject. It also leaves you with little incentive to do further research, and as a result your "instant expertise" can last a lifetime. The internet, I should add, has made it easy for people to learn a little about a subject and has thereby nourished the Dunning–Kruger effect. These days, the world is full of people who, as the result of having read a single article on the internet—or maybe just the title of an article—feel they have a good enough understanding of a subject to share their insights with others.

If those at the pinnacle of the Dunning–Kruger curve continue their studies, though, they become aware of just how much remains to be learned. As a result, their confidence will plunge: See the trough in the middle of the graph. Keep learning, and their confidence will slowly recover—see the right side of the graph—but it is unlikely that it will ever rise to its "instant expert" level. Back then, the person thought he knew practically everything worth knowing about the subject. Now he is painfully aware of how much, despite his efforts, he still doesn't know.

Polymaths and Know-It-Alls

A *polymath* is someone who, as the result of extensive study, knows a lot about lots of things and can therefore be a valuable source of information about a variety of subjects. A polymath will be well aware of the limits of his knowledge, though, and will readily admit as much. A *know-it-all*, by way of contrast, believes he knows everything about something or, in a more extreme case, knows everything about everything.

In some cases, a know-it-all simply *pretends* that he knows everything, in the belief that it will cause others both to admire him and defer to his opinions. Such individuals typically live in fear of being exposed as imposters, and as a result, they might get angry if someone challenges what they say, or indeed, if someone even asks for clarification of what they have said. They will also be reluctant to admit having made a mistake. To do so, after all, would be evidence that they don't know everything. In other cases, a know-it-all isn't *pretending* to know everything; he sincerely believes that he does—or more modestly, that he knows everything about something. Such individuals are likely to be in the clutches of the Dunning–Kruger effect.

A Thinker, as we have seen, will not only realize that she is ignorant of many things but will publicly admit as much. Some will be shocked to hear such an admission and might take it as evidence that she is not very bright, but these critics would do well to rethink this response. Do they really want advice or information from someone who thinks he knows everything? Such a person is almost certainly self-deluded. Furthermore, because he doesn't recognize the limits of his knowledge, he is likely to tell you, with great confidence, many things that simply aren't true. What we should therefore seek is someone who knows the limits of her knowledge, and when we hear her say "I don't know," our estimation of her intellect should rise rather than fall.

People who know a lot about something are susceptible to what might be called *creeping expertise.* Chemist Linus Pauling won a Nobel Prize[2] for his discoveries in quantum chemistry and molecular biology. Late in his career, though, he got the idea that taking megadoses of vitamin C would have substantial health benefits, including preventing and curing colds. He didn't do the experiments necessary to demonstrate that it *did* have these effects; he instead convinced himself, based on his understanding of chemistry, that it *should* have them, and because he was in the thrall of creeping expertise, that was all he needed. He spread his conclusions far and wide. Subsequently, researchers who didn't know much about quantum chemistry and molecular biology, but knew a lot about vitamins and physiology, did the relevant experiments. Their conclusion: Although we need vitamin C to remain healthy, taking megadoses doesn't help us much, and might even hurt us.[3]

Knowledge Reconsidered

People often use "knowledge" and "belief" interchangeably, but in this chapter, I will use "knowledge" in a special way.[4] For our purposes, for a belief to count as knowledge, two conditions must be met: The belief must be true, and you must have good reason to believe it. Thus, although you can *believe* that the moon is made of green cheese, you can't *know* it, for the simple reason that the moon *isn't* made of green cheese. Furthermore, even though a belief is true, it won't necessarily count as knowledge. This is because to know something, you must have good reason for believing it. To better understand this point, suppose that when you ask a friend what time it is, he responds, in an off-hand manner, that he believes it to be 12:00 noon, but adds that because he lacks a watch and cell phone, it is just a guess on his part. Now suppose a witness to this exchange glances at her own watch and announces that your friend is right: It *is* noon. In this case, your friend's belief that it was noon was true, but it would be a mistake to say that he *knew* what time it was. Rather, it was just a lucky guess on his part, and lucky true beliefs don't count as knowledge.

Tell a Thinker that you *believe*, as many creationists do, that the universe was created in 4004 BCE—more precisely, on October 23 of that year[5]—and she might be unfazed: "I don't for a moment doubt that you would believe such a thing." If you instead tell her that you *know* that the universe was created in 4004 BCE, she will likely take exception. Knowledge, she will explain, is true, justified belief. Therefore, to know that the universe was created in 4004 BCE, you must not only believe it, but the belief must be true and you must be able to provide evidence for its truth. Consequently, if you don't have any reasons for believing what you do, or if the reasons you have aren't very convincing, it is an overstatement to say that you *know* that the universe was created in 4004 BCE.

Sometimes people say they know something in order to indicate how confident they are that a belief is true. They might even go further and say that they "know for a fact" that something is true. This is a misuse of language, though. Whether you know something (in the sense that I am using the word) is determined not by how confident you are of its truth but by the quantity and quality of the evidence you can provide to demonstrate its truth. If you believe something but cannot explain why you believe it, you cannot be said to know it. It is instead a "mere belief," no matter how firmly you hold it.

Belief, I would remind my students, is cheap, and because you can form beliefs with little or no effort. Everyone has a head full of them. Knowledge, however, is precious because it takes effort to come up with reasons for believing something to be true. I have characterized Thinkers as individuals whose goal is to fill their mind with true and useful beliefs. I have also said that they need reasons for believing what they do. Consequently, Thinkers can also be characterized as individuals whose goal is to fill their mind with knowledge.

A person can be highly intelligent without being knowledgeable. An intelligent person has the ability to "connect the dots." More specifically, he has the ability to answer correctly the sort of questions that are asked on intelligence tests. Provide him with a body of information, and he can tell you what follows from it. The problem is that he will be as comfortable drawing inferences from a body of false information as he is drawing them from a body of true information. As a result, his mind might end up full of false beliefs—more precisely, beliefs that are "consistently mistaken."

A person can also be knowledgeable without being wise. "Wisdom," in one sense of the word, refers to the ability to apply the knowledge we possess for the good of mankind. Thus, although a person who has spent his life memorizing baseball statistics will know a lot, particularly about baseball, it is unlikely that he will be regarded as wise. Conversely, the great sages of human history didn't know nearly as much about the world as most of us do, but because they were in the possession of a few profound truths and had the ability to share those truths with others, they were—and in many cases still are—renowned for their wisdom.

The Difference Between Being Ignorant, Being Mistaken, and Being Stupid

To be ignorant is to lack knowledge. Consequently, a person who has no beliefs about a subject will be ignorant of it. I, for example, am woefully ignorant of Byzantine history. Ask me a question about it, and I will hold up my hands in despair. The same is true if you ask me about the properties of the subatomic particles known as *charm quarks*, about the mating habits of platypuses, and about the rules of cricket.

There is a difference between being *ignorant* of something and being *mistaken* about it. The former involves a lack of belief, while the latter involves possession of a belief that happens to be false. A case can be made that it is better to be ignorant of something than to be mistaken about it. It is, after all, easier to switch from nonbelieving something to believing it than it is to switch from disbelieving something to believing it. Novelist Leo Tolstoy understood this phenomenon: "The most difficult subjects can be explained to the most slow-witted man if he has not formed any idea of them already; but the simplest thing cannot be made clear to the most intelligent man if he is firmly persuaded that he knows already, without a shadow of doubt, what is laid before him."[6] Because he is in the grip of confirmation bias, the mind of this "most intelligent man" will be closed. He will ignore, dismiss, or twist what we have to say, and as a result, attempts to persuade him will likely be a waste of time.

A Thinker will readily admit her ignorance about many things. She knows that because no one knows everything, everyone is ignorant of something; indeed, nearly everyone is ignorant of nearly everything! Consequently, ignorance is nothing to be ashamed of. She also knows that one of the most important things she can know is the limits of her knowledge. She will therefore agree with Henry David Thoreau, quoting Confucius, that "To know that we know what we know, and that we do not know what we do not know, that is true knowledge."[7] She will also appreciate Defense Secretary Donald Rumsfeld's insightful but widely mocked comment that "there are known knowns: There are things we know we know. We also know there are known unknowns; that is to say, we know there are some things we do not know. But there are also unknown unknowns, the ones we don't know we don't know."[8] A Thinker knows that it is these unknown unknowns that pose the greatest threat. One of her background projects will therefore be to map out her areas of ignorance and to double-check the things that she thinks she knows.

People who are ashamed of their ignorance will be reluctant to utter the words "I don't know" in response to a question, even though they are well aware that they don't know the answer. They might also be averse to asking questions because doing so would reveal their ignorance about a subject. A Thinker will not be similarly reluctant. On the contrary, she might take pride in her epistemic modesty—in the extent to which she knows and admits the limits of her knowledge. It is, after all, a sign that she has made progress in suppressing the ego that would otherwise hinder her ability to optimize her mind.

I have offered Socrates as an example of an ancient Thinker. When asked whether anyone was wiser than Socrates, the Oracle of Delphi responded that "Sophocles is wise, Euripides is wiser, but of all men Socrates is wisest."[9] When this response was reported to him, Socrates was astonished. It subsequently dawned on him that the Oracle was right, but in a surprising way: What made him wise was his recognition of the extent of his ignorance.

Although ignorance is intellectually forgivable, stupidity isn't. To count as stupid, it isn't enough that your mind harbors mistaken beliefs. You must also be in a state of mind that makes it unlikely that you will ever become aware of those beliefs so you can eradicate them. A stupid person won't see any point in looking for his mistaken beliefs because he is smugly confident that there are none to be found. When presented with evidence that challenges one of his beliefs, he might simply shrug it off, or might verbally abuse or even physically attack the bearer of that evidence. He might also double-down in response to the challenge and cling even more tightly to the belief—he might, that is, experience the cognitive bias known as the *backfire effect*.

Willful Ignorance

Besides the general stupidity just described, there is what might be called *selective stupidity* in which a person who is typically eager to learn about the world around him goes out of his way to avoid learning about something, even though it would be easy for him to do and even though, given his interests and values, it is something he *should* be interested in. If we attempt to provide him with information about the thing in question, he will respond by becoming ill at ease. If we don't take the hint and continue providing the information, he might become annoyed and might even break off the conversation. In other words, he will behave about some topics the way a stupid person behaves about most topics.

In an earlier chapter, I described my classroom discussions about chickens. My goal in having them was to reveal an inconsistency that lurked in many of my students' views regarding the morality of fighting gamecocks and the morality of eating broilers. In response to my remarks, some students argued that my account of the lives and deaths of gamecocks and broilers was mistaken, or that there was a morally significant difference between our treatment of gamecocks and our treatment of broilers. When I refuted these responses, though, some students became irritated. It became clear that, in providing them with information about the lives and deaths of broilers, I was telling them something they didn't want to know. And why would students want to remain in the dark about broilers? It is presumably because they enjoyed eating them and because by informing them how broilers came to their plate, I was jeopardizing this enjoyment. From their point of view, I was a real spoilsport.

Willful ignorance of this sort has played a key role in many of history's most disturbing events.[10] Think about the genteel white folk in America's Deep South who refrained from asking obvious questions about the enslaved people who waited on them. Why should they wait on us and not conversely? Did they mind being enslaved? And why did so many of the enslaved women have lighter-skinned children? Furthermore, if they happened to be present when a slave was being beaten, they simply averted their vision—out of sight, out of mind!—or did intellectual somersaults to justify such actions by arguing, perhaps, that Black people felt less pain or weren't fully human.

The cognitive biases described in this and the previous chapter have been with us throughout human history, and in that time have given rise to many mistaken beliefs, some of which had disastrous consequences for humanity. As we shall see in the next chapter, though, the coming of the internet has potentiated these biases, and the coming of artificial intelligence is likely to make matters even worse.

13 | Along Comes the Internet

Meet Boris. He has a head full of beliefs that are simultaneously unorthodox and obnoxious. He is a passionate advocate of multiple conspiracy theories. He is rabidly racist, sexist, and homophobic—oh, and anti-Semitic to boot. He routinely spouts false claims. Sometimes it is because he doesn't realize they are false, but in other cases, he knowingly spreads disinformation because he takes twisted delight in deceiving people.

Before the advent of the World Wide Web,[1] the harm done by Boris—the imaginary individual I have concocted for purposes of illustration—would have been limited. He might have expressed his views at a local bar, where those who heard them might conclude that he was simply venting, drunk, or both. He might also have expressed them at family gatherings, only to have his relatives roll their eyes at his boorishness. If he tried to disseminate his views to a larger audience, though, he would have encountered gatekeepers. The editor of the local newspaper would likely reject his angry, rambling letters to the editor, and the producer at the local radio station would likely decline his repeated offers to appear as a guest.

If Boris simply walked up to someone and unleashed an insult, he might get punched in the nose. With this in mind, he might instead engage in anonymous attacks, perhaps in the form of poison-pen letters, but the impact of such attacks would be far less than if he made them in public. He might therefore engage in smear campaigns in which he tells people lies about his target in an attempt to discredit that person or ruin her reputation. Such campaigns can be successful, but they can also backfire. His target, for example, might discover what he is up to and publicly confront him. In this case, rather than damaging his target's reputation, Boris might himself acquire a reputation for being a spineless weasel.

The arrival of the World Wide Web in the early 1990s would have been a godsend for someone like Boris. It made it possible for him to start a website devoted to his views. On the web, he would encounter neither editors nor producers. If a website host banned him for violating the terms of service, he could simply move to another site with looser terms. He was therefore free to say pretty much whatever he wanted. He could propagate mis- and disinformation, as well as spew hate speech to his shriveled heart's content.

If Boris was too lazy or technologically obtuse to start a website, he could participate on the web forums other people had created. Although many of these platforms are strictly moderated, others aren't, including the 4chan.org website, which is where the infamous QAnon conspiracy theory got its start. These forums can also provide users with a degree of anonymity, making them ideal places to launch smear campaigns. Such campaigns, I should add, make people vulnerable to being doxed,[2] which can have a profound impact on their life and might even result in them becoming the target of physical attacks.

The arrival, in the early 2000s, of social media platforms such as Facebook and Instagram provided Boris with a new outlet for his misanthropy. On these platforms, people would casually tell the world about themselves and in the process of doing so, reveal their insecurities. If he were bored, Boris could spend an afternoon looking for targets. On finding them, he could study their postings and then construct a virtual arrow that would pierce a chink in their emotional armor. Not only that, but the attack would be done in public, increasing its impact and allowing other trolls to pile on with attacks that echoed and amplified those of Boris. The coming of social media allowed Boris and his ilk to inflict substantial emotional pain with minimal accountability.

The Early Internet

What we refer to as "the internet" can trace its roots back to the 1960s. It was initially dominated by tech-savvy individuals who used it as a research tool. With the arrival of the World Wide Web in the early 1990s, though, the internet became much more user friendly and was therefore accessed by a broad range of people. On August 6, 1991, exactly one website existed. It explained what the web was and provided basic instructions for its use.[3] The number of websites subsequently ballooned, and before long the web came to resemble a huge library that lacked a card catalog: The information was there, but where? In response to this situation, internet directories started appearing on the web. They were constructed "manually": People would browse websites and list those that they found useful.[4] As the web grew, though, such directories became increasingly difficult to construct and maintain.

This triggered the development of search engines, the primary component of which was a web crawler, a program that routinely roamed the web and kept track of what it found. In response to a search request, an engine would list the website pages on which it found relevant information. So far so good, but there was a hitch. A search engine's list of results could comprise thousands, millions, or even billions of pages.[5] An engine's web crawler therefore needed to be supplemented with an algorithm that sorted these websites in order of their presumed usefulness to the searcher. In the mid-1990s, many search engines—including Lycos, Excite, AltaVista, and Yahoo!—came into existence, but in 1997, Google developed its superior PageRank algorithm and thereby seized market dominance. Before long, Google (the word) was being used as a verb, and Google (the company) became spectacularly profitable.

And how, you might wonder, can a company make money operating a free website? By keeping track of what people search for, it can learn a lot about them—including what, at the moment they do their search, is uppermost in their mind. It can then display ads on the basis of what it has learned. When someone searches for "coffee machine," for example, the engine might precede its search results with a long list of coffee machine ads. It can also sell information about a searcher's interests to data brokers, who in turn can use it to engage in targeted advertising. As a result, someone who has searched for "coffee machine" might subsequently come across a coffee machine ad while accessing a website about, say, meerkats. What a remarkable coincidence!

Targeted advertising can play a role in convincing you not only to buy a consumer product but to vote for a political candidate.

The coming of the web made it possible for campaigns to gain insight into a voter's personality and intelligence, as well as where she is on the political spectrum. They could also gain insight into her views on various social and political issues, how strongly she holds those views, and in particular, what her "hot-button" issues are. Based on these insights, political operatives could tailor-make ads with her in mind. In 2014, Cambridge Analytica "borrowed" data about millions of Facebook users—without their or Facebook's consent—and used it to engage in targeted political advertising. The resulting ads arguably had an impact on the 2014 American midterm elections as well as the 2016 presidential election.[6]

What are you looking for when you do an internet search? If you ask an objective question like what the capital of Minnesota is, you are looking for the correct answer, namely, St. Paul. If the engine returns an obviously mistaken answer, such as Paris, you will likely abandon that engine as being unreliable. As a result, the engine's provider would lose access to your attention as well as an ongoing stream of information about your interests, and it would thereby forgo ad revenue.

Suppose that instead of asking an objective question, you ask a subjective question, such as whether abortion is morally permissible or how qualified various political candidates are. You might assume that an engine would give everyone who asked a particular question the same results, but this isn't necessarily the case. It might instead give people "customized" search results. You might feel flattered that those responsible for the search engine would go to this trouble on your behalf, but realize that they have an ulterior motive for their behavior: They know that by returning what you take to be agreeable results—maybe because they are factually correct or maybe because they are compatible with your current beliefs—they can increase your use of the engine, which will expose you to more of their ads and provide them with more information about you, which in turn will have a positive impact on their ad revenue. Stated bluntly, they are using you.

Filter Bubbles

By relying on search engines to gather information, you run the risk of slipping into what is known as a *filter bubble*. In that environment, you will be exposed to information that confirms your beliefs, while information that challenges them is filtered out. Life in such a bubble is intellectually cozy; indeed, filter bubbles are to the thought-averse what recliner chairs are to the exercise-averse. Spend too much time in a recliner, though, and you are likely to lose your physical fitness; spend too much time in a filter bubble, and you run the risk of becoming detached from reality.

Filter bubbles can be shared by people, including a married couple, hundreds of cult members, or millions of brainwashed citizens. Those who share a bubble will be remarkably in tune with each other—indeed, so much so that they can complete each other's sentences—but at the same time, they will likely have trouble communicating with those outside their bubble and even worse, with those who occupy "contrary" filter bubbles. Indeed, in this last case, the occupants of other bubbles will seem remarkably uninformed and maybe even crazy. This feeling, by the way, will likely be reciprocated.

Filter bubbles are topic-specific, meaning that a person can be in a bubble with respect to, say, the abortion debate but not with respect to climate change, or vice versa. It is also possible for someone who engages in open-minded critical thinking about most things to slip into a filter bubble with respect to one particular topic. Consequently, even Thinkers are susceptible to the bubble phenomenon.[7] Furthermore, those who reside in a bubble generally don't realize as much. To them, it simply feels like they have a thorough understanding of some aspect of the world. And finally, although filter bubbles existed long before the advent of the internet, its coming has made it easier for people to slip into them, as well as to subsequently take up residence there—which is precisely what many Feelers do.

As we have seen, the coming of the World Wide Web made it easy for a broad range of people to access the internet. It also made it easier for them to create websites. Some created websites that dispensed useful information, while others created websites with entertainment value. Before long, though, the web took a turn for the worse, as an increasing number of bad actors realized its potential for spreading disinformation. Sites providing fake facts and fake news proliferated. Not only that, but someone creating a disinformation website could, with a bit more effort, make it seem more trustworthy by creating ancillary websites that confirmed its claims. Diabolical!

Although bad actors are often the source of disinformation, ordinary people can inadvertently spread it. They might, in particular, share or retweet a fake news item on the basis of its headline, without bothering to read the item.[8] This allows the disinformation to go viral, and as a result, millions of people might be exposed to disinformation that was initially sent to only a few.

Before long, the web was pocked with rabbit holes down which an unsuspecting individual might tumble. In 2016, Edgar Maddison Welch, a twenty-eight-year-old father of two, was surfing the web when he encountered the Pizzagate conspiracy theory, according to which Hillary Clinton and other high-ranking Democratic Party officials were operating a child sex-trafficking ring in the basement of the Comet Ping Pong pizzeria in Washington, DC.[9] On doing further research, Welch became sufficiently convinced of the theory's truth that he felt compelled to take action. He drove from North Carolina to the restaurant to free the children, expose the conspiracy, and maybe become a hero by doing so. Although he had brought guns with him and even fired one of them, no one was hurt. After a brief standoff, he surrendered to police and was subsequently sentenced to four years in prison.

The World Wide Web provided ordinary people with the tech equivalent of a megaphone capable of reaching millions. It also allowed them to spread their messages from behind a cloak of anonymity. They could therefore engage in smear campaigns with minimal chance of retribution. Anonymity also made their messages more believable. If we knew that the source of a message was an unemployed high-school dropout who was still living in his childhood bedroom, we would find his messages laughable, but by posting them on the internet, he could come across as the mysterious source of restricted information.

Another thing to keep in mind is that many of those who are taken in by crazy internet theories had been raised in an environment in which their sources of information—including what they read in books, newspapers, and magazines, as well as what they heard on the radio and television—were generally reliable. As a result, their skeptical instincts are underdeveloped, making them susceptible to campaigns of disinformation. Without intending to do so, technology has immersed intellectually naïve people into an intellectually hazardous environment.

In its infancy, the web was a wonderful source of information. With the passing years, though, it became increasingly polluted with disinformation. These days, someone using the web might feel like a gold miner: Yes, there are nuggets of truth to be found, but you must sift through a ton of sand and gravel to find them. The presence of so much disinformation can be intellectually dispiriting: Why even bother to look for the truth? This is precisely the response that many polluters are hoping to elicit.

The Social and Political Impact of the Internet

We humans are by nature tribal. On the savannas of Africa, we were reliant on the presence and cooperation of others for our survival, and the group we lived and traveled with would have counted as our tribe. For this reason, we are wired to form relationships with other people. In recent millennia, though, the tribal concept has expanded dramatically. You can belong to a political tribe; you can, for example, identify as an American, and as such you might be willing to go to war in defense of your nation. More narrowly, you can identify as being a follower of a certain politician, and once again you might be willing to engage in violent conflict in defense of his leadership. You can also be in a religious tribe, such as Catholicism or Mormonism. And by becoming an ardent fan of, say, the Boston Red Sox baseball team, you can join a sports tribe. This last tribal membership might seem incidental, but it can have an impact on how you spend your free time, as well as on how you dress. It can also give rise to surprisingly powerful emotions: You might find yourself detesting the New York Yankees, as well as their fans. And not to be forgotten, tribal memberships can overlap: It is possible for someone to identify as an American Catholic Red Sox fan.

Tribes have belief systems and, for a Feeler, this can be an incentive to join one. By doing so, he can outsource some of his thinking by adopting the tribe's core beliefs. A Thinker, however, knows that on joining a tribe, she will be discouraged from questioning those beliefs; indeed, asking such questions might result in her expulsion. Because she values her open-mindedness, she will be reluctant to join tribes.

In 1990, a cultural outlier like Boris might never have encountered someone who shared his malignant views about mankind. With the advent of the internet, though, it became easier to find like-minded people as well as to contact them, even though they lived far away. For Boris, such contacts would have been wonderfully reassuring: He was not alone! They also would have increased his confidence in the truth of his beliefs. Before long, he and his online comrades might have formed a virtual tribe that, under certain circumstances, could metamorphose into a mob. This is what happened on January 6, 2021, when people, many of whom had never met in person, converged on the U.S. Capitol to protest what they were convinced was a stolen election.

The internet has come to play a key role in the formation of extremist and terrorist groups. The prime candidates for membership in these groups are lonely, disaffected individuals—mostly young males—who long for social connections and a purpose in life.[10] On joining a group, they will be expected to embrace its principles and do as they are told. It is a proposition that most Thinkers will reject out of hand. Feelers, however, might find it enticing.

For a democracy to function, those in the electorate must have a shared perception of reality. There can, of course, be disputed aspects, but there must be general agreement about what is and isn't real, and about which claims are and aren't true. It is, after all, difficult to come up with a solution to a problem when people can't even agree about its essence. By making it easier for people to slip into filter bubbles, the internet has fragmented reality—or rather, it has fragmented people's perceptions of reality.

The internet has also made it harder for people to resolve disputes. Those who have slipped into a filter bubble will find it difficult to take seriously the claims made by outsiders. It is therefore easy for conversations with them to devolve into personal attacks. People who can't bring themselves to engage in civil conversation will find it difficult to compromise, and without compromise, democracy can't function.

Besides optimizing her own mind, a Thinker will want to help others abandon their mistaken beliefs. As far as the former objective is concerned, the internet is a mixed blessing. Yes, it makes it easier for her to access the information space, but it has also polluted that space. As far as the latter objective is concerned, the coming of the internet—and in particular, social media—has been a curse. By making it easy for people to slip into filter bubbles, it has made it harder than ever to reason with them. That would be bad enough, but as we are about to see, there is reason to think that things will get even worse in the near future.

The Coming of Artificial Intelligence

When I started doing research for this book, artificial intelligence (AI) was something "out there, in the distant future." This notion was shattered, however, by the debut of ChatGPT in November 2022. AI has subsequently come to play a significant role in daily life, and there is reason to think that during the next decade, the world will be transformed by it, and in a manner that will distress Thinkers. To see why, let's consider the impact AI has already had.

Enter a query on a traditional search engine, and it will return a list of useful websites. Enter that same query on an AI chatbot, such as ChatGPT, and it will return a *summary of the contents* of the websites it found. It can also perform assigned tasks. I asked it, for example, to write my bio. It returned a nice little essay, with correct spelling, grammar, and punctuation. In that essay, it asserted five claims about me, only three of which were correct. Google's AI Overviews feature subsequently became the target of ridicule by advising people to use glue to prevent the cheese from sliding off pizza slices, as well as advising them to improve their nutrition by eating rocks.[11]

AI chatbots have since shown dramatic improvement. I recently asked the Perplexity chatbot to "Write a fictional story that contains the following sentences: 'For sale. Baby shoes. Never worn.'"[12] Within seconds, it returned a story that made my eyes well up, even though I knew that it had been written by a (literally) heartless computer. Chatbots can also guide math students through the steps necessary to solve a problem, and in the process of doing so exhibit more patience than most human teachers possess.

Breakthroughs in the development of AI are usually mixed blessings.[13] Yes, students could use ChatGPT to do research for a paper-writing assignment, but they could also use it to write the assigned paper—a paper which, if produced at the last minute, the students themselves might not bother to read. In such a case, students not only won't learn new things but will forego an opportunity to develop their writing skills. Along more serious lines, consider MegaSyn, an AI platform for finding chemical compounds with pharmaceutical potential. Because they were looking for compounds with medicinal value, researchers had instructed the program to exclude toxic compounds by setting its toxicity parameter to 0. MegaSyn returned a long list of promising compounds for them to investigate. And what, researchers wondered, would happen if they switched the toxicity parameter to 1, in which case it would search for toxic compounds? They gave it a try, and by the next morning the program had discovered forty thousand compounds that were potentially as lethal as VX, one of the most toxic chemicals known.[14] And in the same way that AI can be used to find new poisons, it can be used to design deadly viruses.[15]

Some people think of the threat posed by AI in terms of AI robots running amok. More likely, though, it will be people using AI as a tool who are the danger. And does the coming of AI pose an existential risk to humanity? Cases like those just described suggest that it isn't absurd to think so.

AI also poses threats that, although very real, are less calamitous. It can, in particular, be used to create remarkably realistic images of things that don't exist and create videos of events that never took place. This includes videos of people saying (in their own voice) things they didn't say and doing things they didn't do.

Such videos can be used to smear someone, in extortion schemes, or even to convict an innocent individual. We have seen how the coming of the internet has polluted the information space and how, as a consequence, searching for information on the internet is like looking for gold nuggets in low-grade ore. The coming of AI has exacerbated this problem by making it easy to tamper with evidence about what is and isn't the case. As a result, what looks like a nugget of information might turn out to be fool's gold. Realize, too, that the ubiquity of realistic fake videos is likely to make us second-guess the authentic videos we encounter. It will therefore be harder than ever for people—including Thinkers—to stay grounded in reality.

The development of AI will also make us increasingly susceptible to being manipulated by it. As a result of having been trained on data that includes human history and literature, as well as psychological research articles, AI will have a profound understanding of human motivation. Stated bluntly, it will know what makes us tick and, as a result, will be quite proficient at manipulating us, the way a parent is proficient at manipulating a two-year-old child. Bad actors could put this ability to work and thereby affect the choices we make, including not just our consumer choices but those we make at the ballot box.

The sensible way to respond to these dangers would be to take steps to slow down the development of AI and to construct "guardrails" to prevent it from getting too smart too fast. It is unlikely, however, that we will take such steps. This is because we are in the tech-equivalent of an arms race: Companies and countries that are slow to develop AI will lose out to those that push on despite the risks of doing so, and the winners of the race will subsequently have the upper hand.

By historical standards, present-day humans are remarkably smart—smart enough to have invented and deployed the World Wide Web and social media, and then smart enough to invent and deploy AI. When all is said and done, though, it might turn out that we were too smart for our own good. We like to think that we represent the pinnacle of the evolution of life, but we might instead be, in the words of AI researcher Geoffrey Hinton, "just a passing phase in the evolution of intelligence."[16]

But enough of this hand-wringing! Although a Thinker will acknowledge the danger posed by AI, she realizes that she's in no position to prevent its development and will respond accordingly. First, she will take steps to prevent AI from distorting her perception of reality. She will also resist the temptation to outsource her thinking to AI platforms.[17] Second, she will pay close attention to the impact AI is having on those around her. It is likely that in the future, they will become increasingly detached from reality. This detachment, however, will be part of the reality that, like it or not, she must deal with. It is one thing to deal with Feelers who are grounded in reality; it is quite another to deal with those who can best be described as delusional.

PART V

Intellectual Self-Transformation

14 | Mindcare

A Thinker, as we have seen, will be engaged in a mind-optimization program, the goal of which is to fill her mind with true beliefs so she can stay grounded in reality. The first component of this program is a *mindcare regimen* in which she takes steps to reduce her chances of acquiring mistaken beliefs, and the second component is a *mindcleaning regimen* in which she tracks down and eradicates the mistaken beliefs that lurk in her belief set. You might think that this second component wouldn't be necessary—that if a Thinker takes care in acquiring beliefs, there wouldn't be any mistaken beliefs to eradicate—but this is not the case. For one thing, it is unlikely that she would have implemented her mindcare regimen before reaching adulthood, and by then she would have acquired many mistaken beliefs. Furthermore, the belief-filtering mechanism she ultimately adopted was probably imperfect, meaning that mistaken beliefs would sometimes slip past her guard. A Thinker will therefore make a point of finding and eradicating such beliefs.

Suppose, however, that her filtering mechanism *was* perfect. Although new mistaken beliefs wouldn't enter her mind, some of the true beliefs that resided there could become false because of changes in the world around her. Thus, although her belief that

Elizabeth II is queen of the United Kingdom had been true her whole life, it became false when Her Majesty died. It is also likely that a Thinker's true beliefs will periodically give rise to false beliefs, perhaps as the result of fallacious inferences drawn by her. Furthermore, it is possible that as a result of confirmation bias, she will become overly confident of the truth of a belief. On finding such a belief, she won't eradicate it but will adjust her level of confidence with respect to it.

In this chapter we will examine a Thinker's *mindcare* regimen, and in the two subsequent chapters we will examine the *mindcleaning* regimen she uses to find and eradicate her mistaken beliefs, and the *mind expansion* regimen she uses to explore the world around her in search of new beliefs that are both true and useful.

Where to Turn for Information

Suppose that while hiking through a forest, you run out of water. In your search for more, you should avoid drinking water from puddles, and in particular puddles on paths that have been used by animals. That water, after all, would likely be muddy and might be contaminated with germs and parasites. It would be much better to get your water from a clear-running stream. A Thinker will be similarly choosy in selecting her sources of information. She will seek those that are reliable and avoid those that are likely to be polluted with mis- and disinformation. Whereas ingesting polluted water would endanger her physical well-being, accessing mistaken information would endanger her intellectual well-being. Let us, therefore, assess the reliability of various sources of information.

Other people. A Thinker knows that although other people are a handy source of information, their reliability will vary. Furthermore, she will judge a person's reliability not by his level of confidence but by his willingness and ability to explain why he holds the beliefs he does. And finally, when someone characterizes a claim as being "common sense," a mental alarm will sound in a Thinker's mind. In offering this characterization, after all, the person could be attempting to intellectually bully her—the implication being that because the claim is commonsensical, only a fool would challenge it, meaning that she would be foolish to challenge it. One possible response to such an individual: "If what you claim is indeed common sense, you will have no problem defending it, so let's hear what you have to say."

The internet. A Thinker will employ the internet in her search for information, but she knows that, like people, websites differ greatly in their reliability. She will therefore vet a website before exposing her mind to its contents. The first step is to find out who is behind the website, which can be done by clicking on the site's "About us" or "Contact us" tabs. If these tabs are missing, she will be suspicious, and if it turns out that an advocacy group runs or funds a site, she knows that there is a good chance that its content will be biased or even intentionally misleading. Suppose she determines that a site is reliable; indeed, suppose she comes away convinced that it is operated by a fellow Thinker. Even then, it makes sense for her to access multiple sites in her search for information: Thinkers can, after all, disagree about a subject. Also, by seeing what various Thinkers have to say, she can gain a more complete understanding of that subject.

Traditional search engines. On a traditional search engine, we enter a search request, and it returns a list of websites that are likely to be useful. A Thinker will employ these engines—but with care. This is because she realizes that those who design them aren't paid to "enlighten" us; they are instead paid to maximize the number of searches we do. They accomplish this in part by exploiting confirmation bias: They tell us what we want to hear. There are, however, steps we can take to get "unbiased" results from a traditional search engine. We can, for example, keep the engine in the dark about who we are and what we believe. This can be accomplished by clearing our browser's cache before accessing a search engine and subsequently not signing in to that engine. Doing this will be cumbersome, though. Alternatively, we can use a search engine that, because it doesn't sell ads and doesn't sell our information to data brokers, doesn't keep track of our searches. Such engines exist,[1] but they have one drawback: Because they don't make money by selling ads and our information, they might charge people to use them. For a Feeler, this will likely be a deal-breaker: Why pay for something that you can get for free? A Thinker, however, will very much want to avoid falling victim to confirmation bias and might therefore regard search engine subscription fees as money well spent.

AI chatbots. Whereas a traditional search engine returns a list of websites that might contain the information we are looking for, an AI chatbot returns a summary of the information found on the websites it accesses. A Feeler will likely welcome chatbots: They are so convenient! A Thinker, however, will be even more cautious using a chatbot than she is using a traditional search engine. For one thing, a chatbot won't necessarily vet websites the way she does when using a traditional engine. Furthermore, in gathering information on which to base its summary, a chatbot will play the role of curator: It will decide which sites to rely on, but what are its criteria for making this decision? In particular, does an engine lean toward finding sites that will confirm a user's beliefs, the way traditional engines might? And after having selected sites to focus on, will the chatbot write a slanted summary of those sites, again with the goal of telling a user what she wants to hear? Because of these concerns, when a Thinker is engaged in a serious research project, she might employ a traditional search engine, and when she does use a chatbot, she will make a point of accessing the sites listed in the summary it provides.

Where to Turn for News

A Thinker knows that to stay grounded in reality, she has to keep track of what is going on in the world around her. Where, though, should she turn for news? Before 1980, her options would have been limited. There was print journalism in the form of newspapers and magazines. The former would likely have delivered news once a day, and the latter once a week. There was also broadcast journalism. In the United States, radio stations might present current news for a few minutes at the top of the hour. This was supplemented by network television shows[2] that, for half an hour each evening, summarized the day's news.

To obtain their news, these sources would have relied on "shoe-leather journalism." The investigative reporters who wore the shoes in question didn't have the luxury of sitting in a coffee shop or a bar to think about what might be going on in the world and why it might be happening, the way many conspiracy theorists do. They instead gathered evidence by going out into the world to answer the basic *who, what, when, where, why,* and *how* questions regarding an event. In some cases, this would require them to personally witness an event as well as take pictures and videos of what they saw and heard. It might mean talking to people who had witnessed it, as well as examining relevant documents, photos, videos, and physical evidence.

Throughout this process, the reporters would maintain a skeptical attitude. Was the evidence they dug up authentic? Had a photo been altered? And if the photo was indeed genuine, did it depict the event in question or was it a misrepresentation? Similar questions would arise with respect to audio and video recordings, as well as documents and signatures. Reporters would also be skeptical of people's testimony. How did they come to know what they claimed to know? What was their motivation for sharing what they knew? Had they been reliable sources of information in the past? Could their information be corroborated? Reporters would even be skeptical of eyewitness testimony. They know, after all, that besides being mistaken about what they are seeing and hearing, people can misremember what they saw and heard.

Newspaper editors would likewise be skeptical. They might quiz reporters about their investigative strategy, as well as the sources on which they relied. In particular, a newspaper editor might insist on being told the identity of someone who provided information on the condition of anonymity.[3] This editorial skepticism would have been mandated by the newspaper's publisher, who wanted not only to maintain the newspaper's reputation for accuracy but to avoid libel lawsuits.

The news environment was transformed by the spread of cable television in the 1970s and the arrival of round-the-clock cable news in 1980, with the Cable News Network (CNN) being the first such outlet in the United States. Twenty-four hours is a lot of airtime to fill, though, and it resulted in an expanded notion of what events count as newsworthy. As a result, viewers were informed of events that previously would have been ignored. Another turning point was the 1987 repeal of the Fairness Doctrine, which required broadcasters to present different viewpoints with respect to controversial issues of public importance. This gave rise to talk radio, in which blatantly one-sided political commentary was often the mainstay. The arrival of these shows allowed millions of listeners to slip into intellectually cozy filter bubbles, which in turn increased the political polarization of America.

The coming of the web in the early 1990s also had an impact on journalism. Traditional media realized that the web potentially posed an existential threat: Why pay for a newspaper and wait for it to be delivered when you can access the news immediately and for free on the web?

Consider the expenses associated with publishing printed newspapers. Reporters must be paid, and their investigative expenses must be covered. Editors likewise must be paid, as do their higher-ups. Printing and distributing the resulting physical newspapers is quite costly. By going online, though, publishers can dramatically reduce their expenses. The cost of doing shoe-leather journalism remains, and there is the cost of running a website, but this last cost is minuscule compared to the cost of printing and distributing newspapers. Not only that, but by going online, publishers can gain younger readers for whom the idea of subscribing to a print newspaper would seem hopelessly outmoded. And so it was that in the mid-1990s, newspapers with print editions added online editions, in the hope that at some point in the future, the production of printed papers could be abandoned.[4]

The appearance of online news websites gave rise to news aggregators. Rather than researching and writing stories, aggregator websites provide links to the stories posted on news websites. They get their content for free and make money by selling ads that appear alongside the news links they provide. In the mid-1990s, there were only a few aggregators, including the Drudge Report and Yahoo! News. There is currently an abundance of them, with those on Facebook and Google News being particularly popular. There are also niche aggregators that focus on news about, say, business, science, technology, and religion. News aggregators are convenient, update routinely, and are drawn from a wide variety of sources. And not to be forgotten, most of them are free. For this reason, many people turn to aggregators for some or all of their news.

A Feeler probably takes little interest in hard news, preferring instead to focus his attention on sports and entertainment news. And when he does take an interest, he will turn to a source that is likely to confirm his beliefs. He might, for example, read a politically slanted newspaper or news aggregator, or turn to a politically slanted news show on broadcast media or the internet. Because a Thinker wants to stay grounded in reality, though, she will take an active interest in hard news. To determine the accuracy of a news source, she could fact-check the articles it provides by using a fact-checking website,[5] but that would be a tedious undertaking. An alternative strategy is to focus her attention on the process by which outlets gather and report news. She can, in particular, restrict herself to relying on sources that engage in the shoe-leather journalism I have described. It isn't a perfect way to gather the news—some stories will turn out to be mistaken—but given human limitations, it is presently the best way known, and because Thinkers are realists, they will regard this as an acceptable compromise.

15 | Mindcleaning

Occupy a dwelling, and it will periodically need to be cleaned. In most cases, this will involve tidying up, dusting, and washing, but in the case of a hoarder, it will require a large-scale removal of junk. Much the same can be said of your mind. Over the years you have "occupied" it, you have acquired false beliefs. They might have slipped past your critical guard. They could also be the result of fallacious inferences being drawn from true beliefs, or of true beliefs becoming false as a result of changes in the world around you.

A Thinker will realize as much and will therefore make a point of *mindcleaning*, that is, of periodically looking for her mistaken beliefs and eradicating those that she finds. And before moving on, let me emphasize that there is a difference between mindcleaning and what is known as *brainwashing*. In this last activity, someone fills your mind with false beliefs; in mindcleaning, you find and remove false beliefs. Mindcleaning is therefore a remedy for having been brainwashed.

Many people are reluctant to houseclean because of the time and effort it requires. Mindcleaning also takes time and effort, and as a result, it is easy to put off cleaning your mind. Other factors are at work, though. We have seen that many people don't like to think. Mindcleaning requires not just thinking but *re*-thinking—thinking *again* about things we already thought about, meaning that our previous thinking was to some extent wasted effort. *Groan!* Also, in the same way that a hoarder is emotionally attached to what we regard as the junk in his house, we are emotionally attached to many of our beliefs. Because a Thinker's goal is to fill her mind with true beliefs, she will be willing to invest the time and effort necessary to mindclean. A Feeler won't be similarly motivated, and as a result, his mind might be chock-full of beliefs that are not just mistaken but dangerously so.

Cleaning a house is a major undertaking, but cleaning your mind is harder still. This is because at the same time as you are finding and eliminating mistaken beliefs, new mistaken beliefs are appearing. Consequently, in much the same way as a homeowner will divide his housecleaning into manageable tasks—maybe just straightening up one room, one corner of one room, or one drawer of the dresser in that room—a Thinker will mindclean in a selective manner.

Mindcleaning Priorities

The sensible way to initiate a housecleaning project is to assess the mess. If your kitchen is so dirty that it stinks and so messy that you can no longer cook in it, cleaning it should be high on your to-do list. It is perfectly understandable, though, for you to put off straightening up that closet in the unused back bedroom of your house. Similar reasoning can be employed in your mindcleaning activities. Rather than embarking on a random search for mistaken beliefs, you should examine those that play a significant role in your worldview and daily life. A Thinker will therefore commence her mindcleaning by turning her attention to beliefs in "suspect categories," among which are the following.

Beliefs she has "inherited." When she was a child, a Thinker's parents told her what to believe about many things, and she dutifully complied. Even though she loves her parents and might be emotionally attached to the beliefs they planted in her, a Thinker will spend time and effort reconsidering them. For one thing, there is a chance that her parents didn't acquire their beliefs in a thoughtful manner. They might instead have outsourced their thinking to the crowd or to their ancestors. If her parents are still alive, a Thinker can ask why they hold the beliefs they do, and if they provide convincing reasons, she can confidently retain those beliefs, but if her parents have passed away or if the reasons they provide aren't persuasive, she owes it to herself to rethink many of her inherited beliefs. As we saw in an earlier chapter, inherited religious beliefs are a prime candidate for rethinking. So are the moral beliefs she inherited, along with any ethnic grudges she might have inherited. A Thinker has only one life to live, and it would be foolish to spend that life repeating her parents' mistakes.

Beliefs she feels certain are true. As we have seen, there are statements we can be certain are true, including the mathematical claim that "$1 + 1 = 2$," the logical claim that "John is either married or not married," and the semantic claim that "All bachelors are unmarried." In most other areas, though, if we feel certain that a statement is true, we are guilty of overconfidence. A Thinker knows how seductive feelings of certainty can be. (Holding them, after all, absolves us from having to think more about a subject; this, presumably, is one reason Feelers tend to be cocksure of their beliefs.) When a Thinker detects such feelings in herself, she will therefore make a mental note to take a closer look at them. Maybe she should reduce her level of confidence in a belief, and instead of saying "I'm certain that . . . ," she should say "I'm almost certain that . . ." or "I'm highly confident that . . . ." And in some cases, after carefully rethinking a belief she feels certain is true, she will conclude that it is in fact mistaken and will therefore abandon it.

Beliefs that are too easy to defend. Lots of people take the fact that a belief is easy to defend as evidence of its truth, but a Thinker will be suspicious of such beliefs. She expects it to take effort, maybe even considerable effort, to come up with evidence and inferences in support of a belief. When this is not the case, it might be because the belief is in some manner defective. Along these lines, consider again the claim that "Whatever happens is God's will." Yes, this claim is easy to defend, but only because it isn't "falsifiable" in the manner described in Chapter 3. It is therefore a claim that, rather than asserting, a Thinker should dismiss out of hand. A Thinker also knows that those who have been seduced by conspiracy theories can easily defend them. Provide such an individual with evidence that his beliefs are mistaken, and he might respond by accusing you of being in on the conspiracy.

Popular beliefs. Because she is independent minded, a Thinker will be used to holding unpopular beliefs. She will therefore find it a bit unsettling to discover that one of her beliefs is shared by the Feelers around her. Perhaps it is a sign that she has gotten intellectually lazy, and instead of thinking for herself, she is letting others think on her behalf. It might also be a sign that she has capitulated to social pressure: Maybe the Thinker has adopted a popular belief not because it is true, but so she can avoid the disapproval of those around her. She might therefore, as part of her mindcleaning activities, make a point of reassessing some of the popular beliefs she holds.

Beliefs that are the result of "fast thinking." As we have seen, we engage in both fast and slow thinking. Whereas slow thinking is deliberate, systematic, and arduous, fast thinking is quick, effortless, and spontaneous. By way of illustration, we resort to slow thinking to convert Celsius degrees to Fahrenheit—when a cell phone isn't available to do it for us!—and we rely on fast thinking to tell us which of two objects in our field of vision is farther away, as well as what those objects are. Thinkers and Feelers will employ both kinds of thinking; indeed, because of how they are wired, they cannot help but do so. They will likely differ, however, in their reliance on these two thought processes. Whereas a Feeler will appreciate the way fast thinking allows him to form beliefs without conscious thought, a Thinker won't mind engaging in conscious thought. A Thinker will also be more likely than a Feeler to question the beliefs that result from fast thinking. Consider, in particular, the impressions she forms on meeting someone new. A Thinker knows that these impressions, which are the result of wired-in fast thinking, can be mistaken. She will therefore make a point of rethinking them and, as a result, might go out of her way to give a second chance to someone she initially disliked. Thinkers will also make a point of rethinking generalizations they hastily formed about groups of people.

Stress Testing Beliefs

One way to rethink a belief is to engage in a "self-debate": You think about how someone who holds the opposite view on a topic would challenge your belief and then think about how you would respond to that challenge. As a result of doing this, you might come away confident of your ability to defend your views, but this confidence would be unmerited. What you are doing in a self-debate, after all, is the intellectual equivalent of playing a game of chess against yourself. Your ability to "win" such a game is a terrible way to judge your chess-playing ability. A vastly better way to reexamine a belief is to *stress test* it by interacting with someone who not only holds the opposite belief but is capable of providing the evidence and describing the reasoning that led her to do so. Thus, if a Thinker is on the pro-choice side of the abortion debate, the ideal interlocutor for a stress test would be a fellow Thinker who holds pro-life views. A Thinker knows that because Thinkers can disagree, it is entirely possible that such a person exists.

Once this "contrary Thinker" has been chosen, the stress test won't take the form of a public debate in which points are scored and a winner is declared. It will instead be a conversation in which each side explores the views of the other. On what evidence are they basing their views, and what is the thought process by which they arrive at their conclusion? It is possible that the Thinker will come away from this encounter still holding her original views, but it is more likely that her views will have been affected. She might, in particular, have modified her original beliefs or become less confident of their truth. More dramatically, she might have moved a belief into her nonbelief category or might even have concluded that it is mistaken. In this last case, rather than feeling bad about having "lost the debate," she will take consolation in the fact that she has discovered and eradicated a mistaken belief. She is capable of feeling this way because her goal in conducting the stress test is not ego gratification but mind optimization.

Even if a Thinker comes away from a stress test still holding her original belief, she will benefit from having defended it. Hold a belief for a long time, and there is a danger that we will forget why we believe it. We will, in particular, forget the evidence and inferences that led us to that belief. In such cases, our belief will have deteriorated into what philosopher John Stuart Mill derides as "dead dogma."[1] He explains that "He who knows only his own side of the case knows little of that. His reasons may be good, and no one may have been able to refute them. But if he is equally unable to refute the reasons on the opposite side, if he does not so much as know what they are, he has no ground for preferring either opinion."[2] By stress testing a belief in the manner I have described, we are forced to recollect our reasons for holding it, and in the process of doing so, we can "rejuvenate" that belief.

What if a contrary Thinker isn't available to help us stress test a belief? Fortunately, there are other ways to find out what these individuals think. They might have written books or articles in which they explain and defend their point of view, in which case we can read what they have written. It isn't as good as having a chat over a cup of coffee, but it is nevertheless an effective way to expose ourselves to thoughtful dissent. We can also listen to lectures given by such an individual. Best of all, we can listen to a podcast interview in which one Thinker explores a topic with a contrary-minded Thinker. Although the internet has done a lot of intellectual damage, it has made possible the existence of "Thinker podcasts" regarding a number of subjects.[3] Hallelujah!

In many college classrooms, particularly in the liberal arts, instructors explore a controversial topic by engaging in self-debate in front of their students. They express their own view, tell their students the sorts of things the other side of the debate would likely say in response, and then refute those responses. This, they assume, is what it means to consider both sides of the debate, and they might cite this as evidence that they are not simply indoctrinating their students. Mill, however, rejects this assumption. For the debate to be meaningful, he says, students need to hear the contrary views from "persons who actually believe them, who defend them in earnest and do their very utmost for them."[4]

Self-debate is better than no debate at all, but it is a pale approximation of having students listen to a thoughtful adversary. In response to this criticism, the self-debating professor might point out that no one in his department thinks differently than he does on a particular subject, meaning that he has no choice but to engage in self-debate. That such circumstances exist, however, might be evidence that his university isn't particularly interested in transforming students into Thinkers; indeed, just the opposite. Furthermore, he *does* have another choice: He can have his students read or listen to an "outsider" who thoughtfully disagrees with him.

A Thinker might come away from a stress test more confident of the truth of a belief. More often, though, her level of confidence will diminish and, in some cases, she will feel compelled to abandon her belief—good riddance! Perhaps her most common reaction to a stress test, however, will be to refine her belief. If, for example, the belief involved a generalization, she might weaken it by including exceptions: "Abortion is morally impermissible *except when* . . . ." And if it is a belief about causation, she might introduce other causal factors.

Feelers, as we have seen, will dismiss or even insult those who challenge their beliefs. This is unfortunate because a challenger's views might be correct and listening to them could help Feelers eradicate their mistaken beliefs. Thinkers, by way of contrast, not only tolerate challengers but seek them out, and the smarter they are, the better. Thinkers know that beliefs grounded in reality will hold up under scrutiny. They are therefore perfectly willing, as part of their mindcleaning process, to put their beliefs to the test.

16 | Mind Expansion

A Thinker, as we have seen, consciously engages in open-minded critical thinking in an attempt to optimize her mind. The mindcare and mindcleaning regimens described in the previous two chapters foster a critical mindset. To foster open-mindedness, though, a Thinker will supplement these activities with a *mind-expansion* regimen. Whereas mindcare and mindcleaning will slow the growth of a Thinker's belief set and might even shrink it, her mind-expansion regimen will facilitate the acquisition of new beliefs.

To expand her mind, a Thinker will consciously expose herself to new ideas, theories, and perspectives. Furthermore, her goal won't be the acquisition of random facts. What she seeks are new true beliefs that will help her stay grounded in an ever-changing reality. This in turn will not only help her function in daily life but increase her chances of flourishing in life. The following will be among her mind-expansion activities.

Broaden her exposure to news sources. We have seen that a Thinker will be careful about which news sources she exposes herself to. She will, in particular, focus her attention on sources that engage in "shoe-leather journalism." She knows, however, that because they are only human, reporters, editors, and publishers are likely to have biases. She will therefore make a point of relying on multiple sources of news. If she reads the (slightly left-leaning) *New York Times*, she might also read the (slightly right-leaning) *Wall Street Journal* for political balance. And to attain globally balanced news, she might include, say, *The Guardian* (in the United Kingdom) and *The Times of India* in her daily reading. She can also watch the English-language broadcasts of foreign new services on YouTube, or watch foreign-language news broadcasts with closed-captioning and English translation turned on. And to round out her understanding of the news, she might make a point of listening to podcasts and watching shows in which thoughtful, well-informed people discuss current events from different perspectives.

Taking this approach, however, will require considerable time and effort. A Thinker might therefore bypass specific newspapers and magazines in favor of a news aggregator, but she will choose it with care. What she seeks, ideally, is an aggregator that selects articles from sources around the globe. Furthermore, the sources in question should not only rely on shoe-leather journalism but see things from differing political perspectives. It is also helpful if an aggregator identifies those perspectives: Is it a centrist source, or does it lean left or right? By accessing such an aggregator,[1] a Thinker can develop a reasonably complete and balanced understanding of what is going on in the world. At the same time, though, she might worry that on being informed of sources' political leanings, confirmation bias will kick in and she will start ignoring aggregated articles from some sources and gorging on articles from others. She would therefore make a conscious effort to prevent this from happening.

Find and deal with her blind spots. We have encountered the *willful ignorance* phenomenon, in which people actively avoid learning more about some aspect of their life. A Thinker will acknowledge her susceptibility to this phenomenon and will therefore be on the lookout for any intellectual blind spots she might harbor. She will, in particular, make a point of monitoring her thought processes during conversations. When she realizes that she is tuning out information that her interlocutor is providing, she will make a mental note of this reluctance to listen. If it is because she has good reason to think that the information in question is mistaken, her behavior makes perfect sense. Suppose, though, that she is tuning it out because she knows that if she pays attention to it, she will have to rethink some aspect of her life. When she catches herself doing this, a Thinker might devote some of her mind-expansion time to learning more about whatever it is that she is hiding from.

Develop a multi-perspective mindset. We have already examined the role ideologies can play in our thinking and the manner in which they can take our mind captive. If a Thinker relies heavily on one ideology in her explanation of how the world works, she might make a point of spending mind-expansion time exploring contrary ideologies. If she is a thoroughgoing capitalist, she might take a look at Marxism, and conversely; and if she is a thoroughgoing feminist, she might investigate masculinism, and conversely. As a result of these explorations, she might abandon an ideology or even switch ideological allegiances. Even if she ends up retaining her initial ideology, though, her exploration of contrary ideologies will help her attain a fuller understanding of the world.

A Thinker might also, as part of her mind-expansion regimen, spend time trying to look at the world from other people's perspectives. How does the world look to someone who is older than her, to someone of the opposite sex, to someone who is impoverished, or to someone who is disabled? By developing her ability to see the world "through other people's eyes," she can develop her empathic ability, which in turn increases the chance that she will do right by others.

Explore her world. Travel, as they say, broadens the mind. Not only that, but as Mark Twain observed in the conclusion to *The Innocents Abroad*, "Travel is fatal to prejudice, bigotry, and narrow-mindedness, and many of our people need it sorely on these accounts." Travel to another country, and a Thinker will become painfully aware of the extent to which her beliefs are an accident of birth. And besides exploring her world geographically, a Thinker will explore it intellectually by going out of her way to associate with experts and specialists of various sorts. Walk through the woods in the company of a biologist, and she will *see* things that had always been there, right before her eyes. Repeat that walk in the company of a geologist, and she might become aware that what she had formerly dismissed as a curiously shaped pebble is in fact a four-hundred-million-year-old crinoid fossil that lived in a tropical sea. Amazing!

Find and listen carefully to Thinkers, especially to those who are iconoclasts. A Thinker, as we have seen, will turn to contrary Thinkers as part of her mindcleaning activities: They will play a key role in stress testing her beliefs. Even when a Thinker hasn't formed a belief about a subject, though, she will have an interest in what her fellow Thinkers think about it. There is, after all, a good chance that their beliefs are correct, or at least on the right track. But when a Thinker wants, as part of her mind-expansion regimen, to expose herself to radical new ideas, she will look for iconoclastic Thinkers. These are individuals who, as the result of evidence-based systematic thinking, have been led to unconventional conclusions. In particular, when she encounters a Thinker who is advocating a conspiracy theory, she will pay careful attention.

Explore Feelers' minds. As part of her mindcare regimen, a Thinker will make a point of avoiding the stream of disinformation that is spewed by Feelers. The fear is that some of those views will slip past her critical guard and infect her belief set, thereby making it harder for her to stay grounded in reality. At the same time, though, a Thinker knows that Feelers' mistaken beliefs can have a profound impact on the world. She will therefore, as part of her mind-expansion regimen, spend time figuring out what the world's Feelers are up to and what, if anything, can be done to prevent or at least mitigate the harm they might do by acting on their beliefs.

By routinely engaging in mindcare, mindcleaning, and mind expansion, a Thinker increases her chance of optimizing her mind—of filling it, to the extent possible, with beliefs that are true and useful. Realize that these efforts are likely to have an impact on her personality. In the next chapter, I will describe the character traits and intellectual propensities of a typical Thinker. By doing this, I will bring into focus what it means to be a Thinker, so readers can more readily judge their progress toward becoming one.

17 | Portrait of a Thinker

We have seen that to become a Thinker, it isn't enough that you commit to the goal of optimizing your mind; you must also make a conscious effort to achieve that goal. Chances are that you are already making such an effort. In the remainder of this book, I provide material that will help you transition from a person who is merely thoughtful into a full-fledged Thinker. In this penultimate chapter, I provide a portrait of an open-minded critical thinker. More precisely, I describe her distinguishing intellectual and character traits. If you want to become a Thinker, you need to focus on acquiring them. And in the book's ultimate chapter, I present three thought exercises. Doing them will require you to engage in open-minded critical thinking, which in turn will let you assess your potential as a Thinker.

A Thinker, as we have seen, is simultaneously critical and open-minded, but in a specific manner. She won't be critical in the usual sense of the word; she won't, that is, go around making negative comments about things and people. For her, being critical means relying on evidence and reason to decide what to believe and how strongly to believe it. Furthermore, although she will be open-minded, her mind won't be wide open. She will use her critical ability to filter the claims people make. In particular, she will ignore claims made by people who have a reputation for being unwilling or unable to defend their assertions. Listening to such people, after all, would be a waste of time and brainpower.

That said, she will go out of her way to expose herself to outlandish claims made by someone willing and able to defend them. This is because she knows that many of the views that are now widely accepted—such as that germs cause disease, that atoms can be split, and that the Milky Way is only one of billions of galaxies—were at one time regarded as outlandish. She also knows how easy it is to become intellectually complacent and to start thinking that she has everything figured out, meaning that she needn't invest time and effort considering new ideas.

Because she has made an extended effort to think rather than feel her way to conclusions, open-minded critical thinking will have become a Thinker's default mode—or nearly so[1]—and as a result, she will exhibit certain character traits, including the following.

A Thinker is intellectually omnivorous. As we have seen, a Thinker will study natural science to better understand how the physical world works, as well as social science to better understand how people work. This understanding will keep her grounded in reality and thereby increase her ability to predict the future, which in turn will increase her chances of being able to affect it in a beneficial manner. Besides studying science, she will study history to learn its many lessons. And although history doesn't tell her what *will* happen in the future, it gives her considerable insight into what *can* happen, an insight that will play an important role in her decision-making process.

She isn't "opinionated." Because Feelers don't think their way through life, it is easy for them to form opinions. Not only that, but they are likely to be both emotionally attached to those opinions and confident of their correctness. As a result, Feelers often bristle with opinions about a variety of topics. Because Thinkers need to have a good reason to believe something, they will generally be slow to form opinions. Indeed, ask for a Thinker's opinion about a topic that is currently in the news, and she might not have one. It might be that she simply hasn't devoted any thought to the topic, having decided that she has more important things to think about. Alternatively, it might be that as the result of devoting considerable thought to a topic, she knows how complex it is and therefore remains undecided.

She is skeptical. Make a bold claim to a Thinker, and she will ask for supporting evidence. Tell her that "I read it somewhere" or that "It's what they say," and she might ask where you read it or who "they" are. In asking these questions, the Thinker is sizing you up. The world is full of people who are happy to make or repeat bold claims, and a Thinker will want to know whether those claims merit her attention. A Thinker will likewise be skeptical with respect to news reports: Who reported an event, and were there contrary reports? She will even be skeptical about scientific studies. Make a claim about what "studies show," and she will respond that studies rarely "show" something, in the sense of incontrovertibly demonstrating it. At best they provide evidence in support of a claim. Furthermore, on being told what "studies show," a Thinker might ask which studies you are referring to. She might also point out that it is not at all uncommon for scientific studies to disagree. If you instead defend a claim by referring to a single study, she might ask whether it was published; if so, where it was published and whether it was peer reviewed; how the authors of the study did their research; and finally, whether the study has been replicated. Convince her that it is a solid piece of research, and she might point out that it is rare for a single study, no matter how competently done, to establish the truth of a scientific claim. That simply isn't the way science works.

She is comfortable with uncertainty. Feeling certain about something feels wonderful. A Thinker, however, knows that one of the worst things that can happen is for us to feel certain of the truth of a belief that is in fact mistaken. This feeling can give us the confidence to do something tragically stupid. We are therefore better off in the long run if we acknowledge that we live in an uncertain world and believe and behave accordingly. Do this and we will be less likely to act in a precipitous manner. That said, a Thinker will not require certainty before she acts. She knows that, under some circumstances, she will be forced to make important decisions on the basis of limited information.

She is epistemically humble. Many Feelers try to maintain the image that they know, if not everything, then everything worth knowing. As a result, they are reluctant to utter the sentence "I don't know" in response to a question, preferring instead to make up an answer. They are also reluctant to ask questions because doing so would be a tacit admission of ignorance. A Thinker will have no such misgivings, though. She will unhesitatingly admit her ignorance about a subject and will routinely ask questions to fill in the gaps in her understanding of the world. She can behave in this manner because her goal is not to impress other people; it is to optimize her mind.

She is intellectually flexible. A Feeler might take pride in the constancy of his beliefs and look down on people who periodically revise theirs. His reasoning: If your beliefs are true—the way his are—there will be no need to change them. He is also likely to be emotionally attached to his beliefs because he was led by his heart and gut to hold them. A Thinker, however, will be quite willing to change her mind as a result of acquiring new information or becoming aware of a mistake in her belief-formation process. She might, as we have seen, change from believing something to nonbelieving or even disbelieving it, or she might continue to believe something but adjust her level of confidence with respect to it. By behaving in this manner, she dramatically increases her chances of staying grounded in reality.

She is comfortable with complexity. A Thinker knows that a key obstacle to understanding her world is a failure to appreciate its complexity. Consequently, she will resist talking about *the* cause of an event or phenomenon and will instead speak in terms of causal factors. She will also be reluctant to generalize, and when she does, she will likely carve out exceptions. Is abortion morally permissible? It depends on the circumstances. When dealing with a problem, she will consider the possibility that the "obvious solution" has undesirable consequences that aren't obvious, and when making a decision, she will have similar concerns with respect to the "obvious choice." She will also be guarded in the predictions she makes, especially when the human factor plays a role in the events or phenomena in question. She will therefore come across as intellectually subtle, and her beliefs and the claims she makes will often be nuanced.

She is independent-minded. Whereas a Feeler will routinely seek out people to think on his behalf, a Thinker will want to do her own thinking. Yes, she will sometimes rely on expert opinion, but she will choose her experts with care. If her research and thinking lead her to an unpopular conclusion, so be it: She is willing to entertain the possibility that everyone (else) is mistaken about something. Her intellectual independence can cause her to reject conventional labels. Ask whether she is conservative or liberal, for example, and she might say "neither." If you seem perplexed by this answer, she might take you on a guided tour of the political spectrum.

She is open to criticism. When someone criticizes her views, a Thinker won't respond with anger. She knows that for no charge—and maybe with considerable enthusiasm!—her critics look for and point out what they take to be her flaws, weaknesses, mistakes, and inconsistencies. Her friends, by way of contrast, tend to tell her not what she *should* hear but what she *wants to* hear. Consequently, on being criticized, a Thinker might ask her critic to explain where, exactly, he thinks she has gone wrong, and if he can provide a reasonable defense of his criticisms, she might thank him for setting her straight. He has, after all, brought her one step closer to achieving her goal of filling her mind with true and useful beliefs. By responding in this manner, she will be following in the footsteps of Socrates, who describes himself as

> [o]ne of those who would be glad to be refuted if I say anything untrue, and glad to refute anyone else who might speak untruly; but just as glad . . . to be refuted as to refute, since I regard the former as the greater benefit, in proportion as it is a greater benefit for oneself to be delivered from the greatest evil than to deliver someone else.[2]

You might be impressed by Socrates's intellectual humility but realize that an even higher level is possible. Physicist Richard Feynman was passionate in his pursuit of the truth, and when his colleagues proposed a theory, he was eager to look for its flaws—and on finding one, was quick and happy to pounce. And what about when *he* was on the receiving end of such criticism? When physicist Toichiro Kinoshita informed Feynman of a mistake in a paper Feynman had written, Feynman not only took ownership of the mistake but repeatedly apologized for having wasted Kinoshita's time by making it, after which he suggested that they collaborate on a project.[3] A true Thinker doesn't regard contrary Thinkers as enemies or even rivals; she regards them as potential collaborators in a shared quest for the truth.

Even though we can only infer what is going on in other people's minds, their mental mistakes are often glaring—especially if those mistakes affect us personally. You might think our own mental mistakes would be more glaring still because we have a front-row seat from which to observe the workings of our mind. The problem is that despite this excellent seating, our view is routinely obstructed by our ego. It blinds us to our mental mistakes, and as a result we conclude that we make fewer than other people do—or maybe that we make none at all. This allows us to remain blissfully unaware of our mistaken beliefs, and as a result, we can become dangerously detached from reality. We would do well, therefore, to adhere to "Feynman's First Principle": *Don't fool yourself.* And in your attempt to live in accordance with this principle, you need to keep in mind that, in the words of Feynman, "you are the easiest person to fool."[4]

Earlier in these pages, I talked about pure Feelers and pure Thinkers. I argued that pure Feelers exist—indeed, that you were one at three months of age—but that pure Thinkers don't: Because they are human, Thinkers' emotions will periodically interfere with their thought processes. This means that even if you are toward the Thinker end of the intellectual spectrum, you will experience setbacks. When this happens, do your best to learn from them and then boldly continue your intellectual journey.

Because a Thinker does so much thinking about so many things, a Feeler might accuse her of overthinking, but she is unlikely to take offense at this "insult." She knows that because she is intellectually fit (as a result of doing so much thinking) it is far easier for her to think her way to a conclusion than it is for a Feeler. Furthermore, because she is intellectually fit, she might enjoy the process of doing so, the way a physically fit person might enjoy going for a run. A Thinker also knows that, of all the intellectual mistakes she can make, overthinking isn't that bad. The mistake that is really dangerous—and the mistake that Feelers routinely make—is underthinking.

Aspiring Thinkers should regard themselves as works-in-progress: However proficient they are, there will be room for improvement. A key strategy for achieving that improvement is to engage in mindful thinking—also known as *metathinking* or even more grandiosely, as *metacognition*: As we think our way to conclusions, we should watch ourselves think, subsequently reflect on our thought processes, and make a conscious effort to improve them. Bottom line: It takes a lot of thinking to become a Thinker. Did you expect otherwise?

18 | Thinking 101

In these pages, I have explained what is involved in open-minded critical thinking. By now, the Thinker concept has hopefully become, for you, "a thing." It is time to consider your intellectual options. One is to eschew thinking in favor of feeling your way to conclusions. This is the option many people choose, sometimes out of laziness and sometimes because they are unaware of the alternatives. Another option is to resolve to think more and better than you currently do by employing the strategies I have laid out.

The third and most ambitious option, though, is to become a Thinker. You might not feel confident of your ability to make this transition, but there is an excellent chance that it won't be as difficult as you imagine. To help convince you of this, I have devised three thought exercises. By doing them, you can try on the Thinker mantle to check the fit. You can also experience the intellectual satisfaction to be derived from thinking rather than feeling your way toward conclusions. Yes, thinking is hard, but it is also rewarding.

Exercise #1. Form an opinion "from scratch." At present, there is an ongoing, albeit low-key debate about whether municipalities should fluoridate their water supply. Your first exercise is to develop a considered opinion about this issue.

(If you already have one, you will need to choose another topic.[1]) In asking you to form this opinion, I am not asking you to *feel* your way to one; I am asking you to *think* your way. The first step is to do research. This doesn't mean finding a source that discusses fluoridation and adopting its conclusion; it means exploring sources on *both sides of the debate.* You should dismiss sources that make bold claims without offering supporting evidence or that appear to have ulterior motives for making their claims. On completing your research, draw an appropriate conclusion about the fluoridation of municipal water supplies. If you have done your homework, this conclusion will likely be nuanced. Rather than simply declaring that fluoridation is or isn't advisable, you will specify the circumstances under which it is advisable and the circumstances under which it isn't. You will also indicate your level of confidence in the conclusion you have drawn.

Exercise #2. Rethink a belief. In the first exercise, you considered a "new" topic, one about which you had no beliefs. In this exercise, I am asking you to reconsider an "old" topic, one about which you *do* have beliefs. I am asking you, in other words, to *rethink* a current belief. To keep things simple, I want you to examine the following list of widely accepted claims.

From among them, select one that you think is correct.

- Thomas Edison invented the light bulb.
- You shouldn't throw rice at weddings because birds will subsequently eat it, after which it will swell in their stomachs, causing them to get sick and maybe even die.
- For optimal health, you should drink eight 8-ounce glasses of water each day.

Now look for evidence *against* the claim you have chosen. When you have finished Exercises #1 and #2—and not before!—turn to the Appendix for feedback on your efforts.

Exercise #3. Rethink a belief to which you are emotionally attached. Because I don't know you, I can't tell you which belief to rethink. I can, however, offer advice on how to find one. Think about an instance in which a challenge to one of your beliefs made your blood pressure rise or, even worse, made you angry. It is a sign, as we have seen, that you felt rather than thought your way to the belief, and as a result you found yourself emotionally attached to a belief that you have trouble defending. When you have identified such a belief, rethink it by finding a thoughtful, articulate person—ideally a Thinker—who holds the opposite belief. It would be wonderful if you could converse with her, but if this isn't possible, you can read things she has written or listen to lectures or interviews in which she has defended the belief in question. (If you tell me that no such person exists—that those who don't share your belief are stupid and possibly evil as well—it is a sign that you have slipped into a filter bubble. If you want to stay grounded in reality, you need to extricate yourself from it, as well as from any other bubbles that envelop you.) Your assignment is not to *refute* this person but to *learn from* her. As the result of this interaction, you might modify or even abandon your hot belief, and if you continue to hold it, your commitment to it will likely have cooled. In the current social and political environment, that counts as progress.

This, as I have said, is a book about thinking more and better. Although you probably engage in open-minded critical thinking with respect to some subjects, you can expand your intellectual horizons and think carefully about more subjects including, most significantly, social and political issues. There are also steps you can take to think better. You can reassess your sources of news and information. You can reassess your use of surrogate thinkers. You can also examine the impact that your use of social media has had on what and how you think. And not to be forgotten, you can explore your susceptibility to cognitive biases.

Even if you are quite thoughtful, you can probably level-up your thinking. You can, in particular, make a point of relying on evidence-based systematic thinking to form beliefs, solve problems, and make decisions. Yes, it is easier to feel rather than think your way to conclusions, but you will likely pay a price for taking the easy way out: The beliefs you form are more likely to be mistaken, the solutions you come up with are likely to be suboptimal, and you might subsequently regret your decisions. Remember that by thinking rather than feeling your way through life, you increase your chances of staying grounded in reality. This makes it easier for you to deal with the challenges you encounter daily and thereby increases your chances of thriving in this, the one life you have to live.

APPENDIX

In the concluding chapter of this book, I assigned thought exercises. I hope you have completed them because doing so is an excellent way to judge your ability to engage in the evidence-based systematic reasoning that is necessary to play the role of Thinker. It also gives you an opportunity to experience the intellectual satisfaction that comes from thinking rather than feeling your way to conclusions. Here is some feedback on your presumed efforts.

As a result of doing the research for Exercise #1, you likely have a better understanding of the fluoridation debate than 99 percent of people do. Congratulations! Furthermore, the conclusion you formed with respect to fluoridation will be not just an opinion but a *considered* opinion. This might be the first time you have ever held such an opinion. If so, additional congratulations! Not only that, but you have just played the role of Thinker. Why not expand your intellectual horizons and use a similar process to form other opinions?

Invest effort in forming an opinion, and if someone challenges it, your confidence won't be shaken. Indeed, because you have "done your homework," you might understand his side of the issue better than he does, meaning that you can calmly, rationally explain where he went wrong. It is a wonderful position to be in! At the same time, though, you should remain open to the possibility that *you're* the one who made a mistake, and if this turns out to be the case, you can come away from the encounter feeling not humiliated but enlightened.

In the process of developing this exercise, I did my own research. It would appear that I had unwittingly fallen victim to groupthink with respect to the fluoridation debate: I had assumed that because so many municipalities were fluoridating their water supply, there must be good reason for doing so, but on researching the issue, I discovered that although there was a plausible case for fluoridation, the argument *against* it was more robust and interesting than I had imagined. (This is often the case when you investigate a controversial topic.) I also discovered that some of the scientific research on the effectiveness of fluoridation was "tainted." In particular, some of the studies that opposed fluoridation had been funded by companies that manufacture fluoridated toothpaste. In the end, I decided that coming up with a considered opinion about fluoridation of municipal water supplies would take more thought and study. As a result, if you asked me for my opinion on the fluoridation debate, my answer would currently be: "It's complicated"—which, I should add, is a perfectly acceptable conclusion for a Thinker to draw. I would also tell you that whether or not a municipality should fluoridate its water supply depends on its circumstances. In particular, how big is the municipality, does its water naturally contain fluoride, and how affluent are its residents?

Exercise #2 was initially to "Rethink a mistaken belief that you hold," but this assignment was problematic. I would be asking you to come up with a claim that, besides believing, you believed was mistaken—an impossible task. What I needed was a claim that you believed without realizing that it was mistaken, but given that

I know nothing about you, how could I do this? The answer was to list some claims that, although widely accepted, are mistaken or otherwise defective. The assumption was that you believed at least one of them, meaning that by examining it, you would be rethinking a mistaken belief that you hold. Let me describe some of the things you might have noticed in examining these claims.

In determining whether Edison invented the light bulb, you were confronted with the question of what, exactly, counts as a light bulb. Long before Edison, people made wires incandesce by passing electricity through them. Wouldn't these count as primitive light bulbs? Maybe what Edison discovered was not so much *the* light bulb as *a better* light bulb. Conclusion: The claim that Edison invented the light bulb is neither true nor false; it is better described as vague.

The claim that birds swell up and get sick or die when they eat rice seems plausible: Rice, after all, swells when you soak it in water. It is therefore a claim that ought to be true. There is, however, compelling evidence that birds can eat rice safely. The rice claim would therefore appear to be an urban myth. If we fell for this myth, though, there are likely many more that we have fallen for but have not yet discovered so we can eradicate them.

This brings us to the claim that we should drink eight 8-ounce glasses of water each day. This claim is thoroughly embedded in our culture—indeed, I have heard medical professionals make it—but it doesn't seem to be based on proper scientific research. Furthermore, the claim itself is ambiguous. Is the claim that we must specifically drink eight 8-ounce glasses of water? Or is it that, over the course of a day, we should drink 64 ounces of water, maybe not in the form of 8-ounce servings and not on eight occasions? Does drinking soda pop, coffee, or beer, which are mostly water, count as drinking water? And what about the water in the foods we eat. Cucumbers are mostly water, as is soup. Does that water count in meeting the 64-ounce requirement? Furthermore, doesn't the amount of water we need depend on our circumstances? Don't we need more when it is scorching hot outside than when it is icy cold? The claim about needing eight 8-ounce glasses of water daily, then, is at least ambiguous and is almost certainly mistaken. And yet people not only accept it but act on it.

If our goal is to optimize our mind, we should not only assume that we harbor mistaken beliefs but should actively look for them. This is what mindcleaning is about. On discovering a mistaken belief, we should eradicate it, but before doing so, we should take a moment to reflect on what it felt like to hold it—namely, the same as it feels to hold a true belief! We should likewise pause to consider how we came to hold that mistaken belief. We might have heard someone make a claim, and this event somehow planted a "belief seed" in our mind. With the passage of time, this seed—nourished, perhaps, by confirmation bias—grew into a full-fledged belief, at which point we might have shared it with other people. Become a Thinker, and we will become suspicious of what "everyone knows." This in turn will make us less likely to fall for urban myths.

NOTES

Preface
1. Realize that some true beliefs are more valuable than others. In particular, someone whose mind was crammed with correct baseball statistics would have a mind full of true beliefs, but there are doubtless other true beliefs that would be more useful to him in going about his daily business and thriving in life. Because we are only human, we have limited time and energy to gather information, as well as limited ability to remember it. Our goal, therefore, should be to fill our mind, to the extent possible, with beliefs that are not only true but useful, with the utility of a belief depending on our values and circumstances.

Introduction
1. This research resulted in my book *On Desire: Why We Want What We Want* (Oxford University Press, 2006).
2. In making this claim, I am invoking what is known as the *correspondence theory of truth*.
3. If they have been paying attention in class, modern sixth graders know about electricity, bacteria, Australia, and tornadoes. They lack a detailed understanding of them, of course, but they do know about them. Socrates didn't.

Chapter 1

1. For more on this point, see my book *You: A Natural History* (Oxford University Press, 2018), 82–84.
2. Napoleon stood at 5 feet 7 inches, which was above average for the time and place in which he lived. Humans and monkeys evolved from a common ancestor that was neither a human nor a monkey. For evidence that duck quacks echo, watch Bree Barnett Dreyfuss, "Braniac Quack Echo," YouTube video, February 4, 2017, https://www.youtube.com/watch/T9M7KSAJYOc.
3. See, for example, Saint Anselm's *Proslogion*.
4. Some clarification is in order. Earlier I referred to charm quarks. If you asked me to describe them, I wouldn't get far: "They are subatomic particles." Give me a minute or two, though, and I would be able to point you to an authority who can describe these particles in mind-boggling detail. If you are interested in learning more about charm quarks, here is an excellent place to start: Frederick A. Harris, "Charm Quark," *Symmetry Magazine*, May 1, 2009, https://www.symmetrymagazine.org/article/may-2009/charm-quark.
5. The *Merriam-Webster Dictionary* defines *disbelieve* as "not believe," but as we have seen, there are two ways in which you can "not believe" something. In these pages, I will reserve the word *disbelieve* for cases in which you actively believe a statement to be false. Thus, although you disbelieve the claim that Los Angeles is the capital of France, you probably don't disbelieve (in my sense of the word) the claim that Yaren is the capital of the Republic of Nauru.
6. The verb *nonbelieve* appears in neither the *Oxford English Dictionary* nor the *Merriam-Webster Dictionary*. The noun *nonbelief*, however, does appear in the latter dictionary, where it is defined as "absence or lack of belief," which is pretty close to the meaning I am suggesting for the word.
7. Theism can take different forms. Besides the monotheists who believe that only one god exists, there are polytheists and pantheists.

8. Besides "demonstrating" that 5 + 2 = 7, you can mathematically prove it. Doing so, however, is rather complex. Indeed, it took Whitehead and Russell 379 pages to prove "from scratch" the rather simpler statement that 1 + 1 = 2. See Alfred North White and Bertrand Russell, *Principia Mathematica* (Cambridge University Press, 1910).
9. Bertrand Russell, "An Outline of Intellectual Rubbish," in *Unpopular Essays* (Clarion, 1969), 104.

Chapter 2

1. Ullrich Wagner, Pascal Schlechter, and Gerald Echterhoff, "Socially Induced False Memories in the Absence of Misinformation," *Scientific Reports* 12 (May 11, 2022), https://doi.org/10.1038/s41598-022-11749-w.
2. Jordana Cepelewicz, "To Make Sense of the Present, Brains May Predict the Future," *Quanta Magazine*, July 10, 2018, https://www.quantamagazine.org/to-make-sense-of-the-present-brains-may-predict-the-future-20180710/.
3. I was delighted to find this word in the dictionary. If it hadn't been there, I would probably have taken it on myself to invent it, the way I invented *Thinker*, with a capital T. Argufiers, after all, serve as a wonderful foil to Thinkers.
4. Some clarification is in order. The earth isn't truly round. It is instead a slightly irregular oblate spheroid. It is oblate because its diameter from pole to pole is less than its diameter across the equator, and it is irregular because of the mountains and valleys on its surface. For ordinary purposes, though, it counts as "round."
5. Jess Blumberg, "A Brief History of the Salem Witch Trials," *Smithsonian Magazine*, October 23, 2007, https://www.smithsonianmag.com/history/a-brief-history-of-the-salem-witch-trials-175162489/.
6. Heather Rockwood, "Giles Corey, Pressed to Death," *The Beehive*, September 17, 2021, https://www.masshist.org/beehiveblog/2021/09/giles-corey-pressed-to-death/.

Chapter 3

1. Notice that this is not the same as saying that everyone is under ten feet tall because someone who is exactly ten feet tall will fail to be over ten feet tall.
2. The exception is if we are talking about 100 percent or 0 percent of things, inasmuch as these claims, despite making reference to percentages, are universal generalizations.
3. "Bigfoot—Patterson/Gimlin Film," YouTube video, November 27, 2016, https://www.youtube.com/watch/Q60mSMmhTZU.
4. Sarah C. P. Williams, "'Bigfoot' Samples Analyzed in Lab," *Science*, July 1, 2014, https://www.science.org/content/article/bigfoot-samples-analyzed-lab.
5. This claim is only "approximately true." Because of wind resistance, an object dropped in air (as opposed to a vacuum) will reach its terminal velocity, at which point its speed will stop accelerating.
6. Aspects of Newton's law of gravity, for example, were subsequently challenged by Einstein.
7. For the record, I just checked my horoscope online. It advised me to reclaim my right to take care of myself. Good advice! It also predicted that "The moon's link with eccentric Uranus" might help me express myself in a new light. One can only hope!

Chapter 4

1. Remove any single belief, and you break the "chain of belief."
2. If your actions are at odds with private, unstated beliefs, it isn't clear that you count as a hypocrite. You might better be described as weak-willed.
3. Ralph Waldo Emerson, "Self-Reliance" (1841).
4. Duane Cady, "Pacifism Is Not Passivism," *Philosophy Now* 105 (2014), https://philosophynow.org/issues/105/Pacifism_Is_Not_Passivism.
5. For a summary of the medical case against meat consumption, see Lizzie Streit, "Benefits of Not Eating Meat (or at Least Less of It)," *Healthline*, August 27, 2021, https://www.healthline.com/nutrition/benefits-of-not-eating-meat.

6. Son Nguyen, "Hanoi People Lose Interest in Dog Meat," *HanoiTimes*, July 15, 2023, https://hanoitimes.vn/hanoi-people-lose-interest-in-dog-meat-324206.html.
7. Barry Estabrook, "Factory Farm," interview by Lynne Roseto Kasper, *The Splendid Table* (podcast), May 8, 2015, https://www.splendidtable.org/episode/2015/05/08/factory-farm.

Chapter 5

1. The word "polysemous" is an exception. Ironically, its one and only meaning is *having multiple meanings*.
2. When I refer to "the dictionary" in these pages, I will be referring to the *Merriam-Webster Dictionary*.
3. "Run" (used as a verb) has an astonishing 645 distinct meanings. (Notice that $7 \times 645 = 4{,}515$.) "Has 'Run' Run Amok? It Has 645 Meanings . . . So Far," *NPR*, May 30, 2011, https://www.npr.org/2011/05/30/136796448/has-run-run-amok-it-has-645-meanings-so-far.
4. This pun works better when it is spoken rather than written.
5. Daniel Dennett, "The Evolution of Confusion," 36:20–37:00, October 30, 2009, https://www.youtube.com/watch/D_9w8JougLQ.
6. Joshua Rothman, "Daniel Dennett's Science of the Soul," *The New Yorker*, March 20, 2017.
7. Someone can, of course, challenge these claims about morality.
8. There is a move afoot to replace *UFO* with *UAP*, which stands for "unidentified aerial phenomenon," with the latter being a broader term: Any UFO will also be a UAP, but not conversely.
9. To see why I say this, see my book *You: A Natural History* (Oxford University Press, 2018), 82–84.
10. "U-3 vs. U-6 Unemployment Rate: What's the Difference?" *Investopedia*, September 14, 2023, https://www.investopedia.com/articles/investing/080415/true-unemployment-rate-u6-vs-u3.asp.
11. Sarah Fass, "Measuring Poverty in the United States," National Center for Children in Poverty, May 1, 2009, https://www.nccp.org/publication/measuring-poverty-in-the-united-states/.

12. This stipulative definition of racism apparently appeared in the 1970s and subsequently caught on. Some sources suggest that social scientist Patricia Bidol-Pavda introduced the "racism plus power" concept in her book *Developing New Perspectives on Race: An Innovative Multi-Media Social Studies Curriculum in Race Relations for the Secondary Level* (New Detroit, 1970). See, for example, Christopher Estrada-Salazar, "No, Racism Is Not Prejudice Plus Power," *The Student Life*, March 13, 2019, https://tsl.news/opinion-no-racism-is-not-prejudice-plus-power/.
13. Although dictionaries can take a prescriptivist approach and tell what words belong in the language, most modern dictionaries take a descriptivist approach and tell what words are in fact being used as well as how they are being used. Cory Stamper, *Word by Word: The Secret Life of Dictionaries* (Pantheon Books, 2017), 35.

Chapter 6

1. This timing is indicated by Google's Ngram Viewer: https://books.google.com/ngrams/graph?content=pre-owned&year_start=1800&year_end=2022&corpus=en&smoothing=3.
2. This timing is indicated by Google's Ngram Viewer: https://books.google.com/ngrams/graph?content=%22pro-life%22%2C%22pro-choice%22&year_start=1800&year_end=2022&corpus=en&smoothing=3.
3. Amy L. Solomon, "In Search of a Job: Criminal Records as Barriers to Employment," *HIJ Journal* 270 (June 14, 2012), https://nij.ojp.gov/topics/articles/search-job-criminal-records-barriers-employment.
4. Aaron E. Carrol, "Should You Circumcise Your Baby Boy?" *New York Times*, May 9, 2016, https://www.nytimes.com/2016/05/10/upshot/why-science-cant-help-you-much-in-deciding-on-circumcision.html.
5. S. Moses, R. C. Bailey, and A. R. Ronald, "Male Circumcision: Assessment of Health Benefits and Risks," *Sexually Transmitted Infections* 74,

no. 5 (October 1998), https://pmc.ncbi.nlm.nih.gov/articles/PMC1758146/.
6. As a practical matter, such tracing would be difficult or even impossible, so imagine that time travel was an option.
7. We can argue about whether Abraham was the first Jew; indeed, some will argue that Judaism wasn't really a religion until Moses formalized it.
8. It is, of course, debatable whether such visits occurred. Abraham's existence is also debatable.
9. It is also possible that the ancestor switched from having no religion to having one. Furthermore, in saying this, I am assuming that the descendants of the convert would have simply gone along with the convert's decision, but this needn't be the case. I am also simplifying for the sake of argument. There could, for example, have been multiple ancestors who simultaneously switched their religion.

Chapter 7

1. We could talk about *referring* to a word rather than *mentioning* it. By using the latter terminology, I am following standard philosophical practice.
2. There are variations on this practice. You can say "end quote" rather than "unquote." People sometimes say "quote, unquote" before the word in quotes, but this creates confusion if it is a phrase rather than a word that is being placed in quotes.
3. Daniel Dennett, "The Evolution of Confusion," YouTube video (31:15–31:45), October 30, 2009, https://www.youtube.com/watch/D_9w8JougLQ.
4. Philosopher Bertrand Russell uses the rather more complex sentence "Quadruplicity drinks procrastination" to illustrate category errors, and linguist Noam Chomsky uses "Colorless green dreams sleep furiously."
5. Gilbert Ryle, *The Concept of Mind* (Routledge, 1949), 6.

6. Stephen Law, "Pseudoprofundity," *Psychology Today*, June 22, 2011, https://www.psychologytoday.com/us/blog/believing-bull/201106/pseudoprofundity.
7. For an in-depth discussion of the role language plays in the establishment and maintenance of cults, see Amanda Montell's *Cultish: The Language of Fanaticism* (Harper, 2021).
8. Hinton, who is not a physicist, won the Nobel Prize for physics. There isn't a Nobel Prize for computer science.
9. Ashutosh Shrivastava (@ai_for_success), "Geoffrey Hinton, Godfather of AI: 'AI is like a very cute tiger cub. You better be sure when it grows up, it never . . . ,'" X.com, December 29, 2024, 4:01 AM, https://x.com/ai_for_success/status/1873293374960304187.
10. This is the analysis I offer in *You: A Natural History* (Oxford University Press, 2018), 190.

Chapter 8

1. Edward N. Lorenz, "Predictability: Does the Flap of a Butterfly's Wings in Brazil Set Off a Tornado in Texas?" *AAAS Lecture*, December 29, 1972, https://static.gymportalen.dk/sites/lru.dk/files/lru/132_kap6_lorenz_artikel_the_butterfly_effect.pdf.
2. When that first virus replicated, its altered DNA was disseminated; indeed, it literally went viral.
3. Rob Mander, "Redskins Rule: Barack Obama's Victory over Mitt Romney Tackles Presidential Predictor for Its First Loss," *Chicago Tribune*, November 7, 2012, https://www.chicagotribune.com/2012/11/07/redskins-rule-barack-obamas-victory-over-mitt-romney-tackles-presidential-predictor-for-its-first-loss/.
4. Realize that this would be impossible to do because our presence at the time of that event would change many things.
5. Raine Sihvonen, Mika Paavola, Antti Malmivaara, Ari Itälä, Antti Joukainen, Heikki Nurmi, et al. "Arthroscopic Partial Meniscectomy versus Sham Surgery for a Degenerative Meniscal Tear," *New England Journal of Medicine* 369, no. 26 (December

26, 2013), https://www.nejm.org/doi/full/10.1056/nejmoa1305189. For a description of the surgery, along with a video, see "Fidelity Study: Common Knee Surgery Ineffective in Study," February 8, 2016, https://www.youtube.com/watch/RaDWkJHmEB0.
6. James H. Lubowitz, Matthew T. Provencher, and Michael J. Rossi, "Could the *New England Journal of Medicine* Be Biased Against Arthroscopic Knee Surgery? Part 2" *Arthroscopy* 30, no. 6 (June 2014), https://www.arthroscopyjournal.org/article/S0749-8063(14)00285-0/references.
7. For a discussion of the exact wording of this quotation, see "Quote Origin: It Is Difficult to Get a Man to Understand Something When His Salary Depends Upon His Not Understanding It," *Quote Investigator*, November 30, 2017, https://quoteinvestigator.com/2017/11/30/salary.
8. Harri Hemilä, "Zinc Lozenges and the Common Cold: A Meta-analysis Comparing Zinc Acetate and Zinc Gluconate, and the Role of Zinc Dosage," *JRSM Open* 8, no. 5 (May 2, 2017), https://www.ncbi.nlm.nih.gov/pmc/articles/PMC5418896/.
9. An advocate of rats' rights will likely challenge this use of rats. See "Hidden Lives of Rats and Mice," *PETA*, https://www.peta.org/features/hidden-lives-rats-mice/.
10. In these pages I have routinely used the feminine pronoun to refer to Thinkers. I will henceforth use the masculine pronoun to refer to Feelers. I do this not because I assume that only women can be Thinkers or that only men can be Feelers; I do it to simplify discussions.
11. Even though there aren't any pure Thinkers, it is useful for us, when deciding how to live our lives, to employ the pure-Thinker concept. In particular, we can set out to be guided by reason, knowing full well that our attempts will fall short. In Stoic philosophy, reference is sometimes made to "the Stoic sage," who perfectly exemplifies the Stoic virtues. Although it is unlikely that such an individual has existed or ever will exist, invoking him as an archetypal figure

provides aspiring Stoics with a target at which to aim. The "Pure Thinker" figure can play a similar role for aspiring Thinkers.
12. Adam Satariano and Davey Alba, "Burning Cell Towers, Out of Baseless Fear They Spread the Virus," *New York Times*, April 10, 2020, https://www.nytimes.com/2020/04/10/technology/coronavirus-5g-uk.html.
13. Tom Nichols, *The Death of Expertise: The Campaign Against Established Knowledge and Why It Matters* (Oxford University Press, 2024).
14. Neil Francey and Simon Chapman, "'Operation Berkshire': The International Tobacco Companies' Conspiracy," *British Journal of Medicine* 321, no. 7257 (August 5, 2000), https://www.ncbi.nlm.nih.gov/pmc/articles/PMC1118337/.

Chapter 9

1. Words to this effect have been attributed to both Charles Kettering and John Dewey, but I was unable to find a definitive source.
2. This is also known as a *can't-lose* strategy or, more formally, as a *dominant* strategy.
3. An exception might be if the one casualty was the general who brilliantly led the enemy attack.
4. A general's analysis of costs and benefits will likely be more complex than this. In particular, it will take civilian casualties into account.
5. The argument in support of this claim would be a variant of the life-is-precious argument given in conjunction with our discussion of absolute pacifism.
6. It is an overstatement to say that she will do nothing. If the problem is serious, she might redouble her efforts to find a cost-effective solution. She might also start looking for ways, not to solve the problem outright, but to ameliorate its impact.
7. What I am describing here is akin to what political philosopher Jason Brennan refers to as an *epistocracy*. See his book *Against Democracy* (Princeton University Press, 2016).

8. "Poverty and Spending over the Years," Federal Safety Net, https://federalsafetynet.com/poverty-and-spending-over-the-years-2/.
9. Anne Kim, "The Rise of Poverty Inc.: How Helping the Poor Became Big Business," *The Atlantic*, June 1, 2024, https://www.theatlantic.com/ideas/archive/2024/06/corporate-middlemen-poverty-programs/678548/.
10. "Compressed Mortality, 1968–1978 Results, Centers for Disease Control and Prevention," https://wonder.cdc.gov/cmf-icd8.html.
11. Matthew F. Garnett and Arialdi M. Miniño, "Drug Overdose Deaths in the United States, 2003–2023," *NCHS Data Brief*, December 2024, https://www.cdc.gov/nchs/data/databriefs/db522.pdf.
12. For insight into the impact drug-gang violence can have on communities, see "ICE HSI Leads the Largest Street Gang Takedown in New York City History," U.S. Immigration and Customs Enforcement, April 28, 2016, https://www.ice.gov/news/releases/ice-hsi-leads-largest-street-gang-take-down-new-york-city-history.
13. "Offenses," Federal Bureau of Prisons, https://www.bop.gov/about/statistics/statistics_inmate_offenses.jsp.
14. Kevin Sack, "Door-Busting Drug Raids Leave a Trail of Blood," *New York Times*, March 19, 2017, https://www.nytimes.com/interactive/2017/03/18/us/forced-entry-warrant-drug-raid.html. See also Dara Lind, "Cops Do 20,000 No-Knock Raids a Year," *Vox*, May 15, 2015, https://www.vox.com/2014/10/29/7083371/swat-no-knock-raids-police-killed-civilians-dangerous-work-drugs.
15. When thinking about these future generations, though, we need to keep in mind that besides inheriting many of our problems, they also inherit our "wealth." They will, for example, be able to benefit from the roads, canals, libraries, hospitals, and factories we have built. They will also benefit from our inventions, our discoveries, and our literary and artistic output.

Chapter 10

1. According to one study, the average person makes more than two hundred food-related decisions daily. See Brian Wansink and

Jeffery Sobal, "Mindless Eating: The 200 Daily Food Decisions We Overlook," *Environment and Behavior* 39, no. 1 (January 2007): 101–123, https://journals.sagepub.com/doi/abs/10.1177/0013916506295573. This is probably an underestimate, though, inasmuch as it ignores decisions about which of the foods on your plate you will eat next, how big your bite will be, how many times you will chew it, whether you will swallow a beverage to wash it down, and so on.

2. What, you might wonder, is the difference between problem-solving and decision-making? It is a difficult question to answer, in part because these words are used in many different ways. Furthermore, the two activities are usually intertwined: In solving a problem, you must decide which of the possible solutions to implement, and in making this decision, you must take into account the problems to which its implementation might give rise. For present purposes, though, I will treat problem-solving and decision-making as independent activities. Roughly speaking, whereas problem-solving is focused on your current situation, decision-making is forward-looking.

3. For an insightful exploration of this phenomenon, see L. A. Paul, *Transformative Experience* (Oxford University Press, 2014).

4. One notable exception is people with Generalized Anxiety Disorder (GAD).

5. Sometimes an important decision must be made in a matter of seconds, and under those circumstances a gut-level decision is probably better than no decision at all. Having said this, though, I should add that a Thinker will go to great lengths to avoid ending up in circumstances in which she has only a few seconds to make an important decision.

6. In the most common version of roulette, there are the red and black numbers 1–36, plus two green numbers, 0 and 00, for a total of 38 numbers. This means that on a spin of the wheel, there are 37 numbers other than the number 17 that can come up. Divide 37 by 38, and we get a result of 97.4 percent.

7. The source of this story is unclear. My account is based on Alan Watts's telling of it: Alan Watts, "The Runaway Horse," *Official Alan Watts Org*, April 20, 2020, https://www.youtube.com/watch/QmYG 0LIznkk.
8. Besides practicing Stoicism, I write about it. See my *Guide to the Good Life: The Ancient Art of Stoic Joy* (Oxford University Press, 2009) and my *Stoic Challenge: A Philosopher's Guide to Becoming Tougher, Calmer, and More Resilient* (W. W. Norton, 2019).
9. Marcus Aurelius, *Meditations*, trans. Gregory Hays (Modern Library, 2003), book 5, 53.
10. Seneca, *Letters from a Stoic*, trans. Robin Alexander Campbell (Penguin Putnam, 1969), letter XI, 56.

Chapter 11

1. Those seeking more information are encouraged to look at Daniel Kahneman's *Thinking, Fast and Slow* (Farrar, Straus and Giroux, 2011).
2. The word "confirm" is ambiguous. It can mean *conclusively prove that a claim is true*, which will be the case only under special circumstances. It can also mean *be supportive of a claim without conclusively proving it*, which is what is going on in cases of confirmation bias.
3. For a discussion of the impact confirmation bias has on science, see Chris Lee, "Confirmation Bias in Science: How to Avoid It," *Ars Technica*, July 13, 2010, https://arstechnica.com/science/2010/07/confirmation-bias-how-to-avoid-it/.
4. Chittaranjan Andrade, "HARKing, Cherry-Picking, P-Hacking, Fishing Expeditions, and Data Dredging and Mining as Questionable Research Practices," *Journal of Clinical Psychiatry* 82, no. 1 (February 18, 2021), https://www.psychiatrist.com/jcp/harking-cherry-picking-p-hacking-fishing-expeditions-and-data-dredging-and-mining-as-questionable-research-practices/.
5. According to the dictionary, a *feminist* is someone who believes in and advocates "the political, economic, and social equality of the sexes expressed especially through organized activity on behalf of women's

rights and interests." A man can believe and advocate this, meaning that a man can be a feminist, in this sense of the word. Along similar lines, a woman can be a masculinist.

6. Oksana Leukhina and Amy Smaldone, "Why Do Women Outnumber Men in College Enrollment?" *Federal Reserve Bank of St. Louis: On the Economy Blog*, March 15, 2022, https://fraser.stlouisfed.org/title/economy-9397/women-outnumber-men-college-enrollment-687253.

7. This is what, back in Chapter 6, we referred to as *discrimination*^{1}.

Chapter 12

1. Alexander Pope, "An Essay on Criticism," *Poetry Foundation*, October 13, 2009, https://www.poetryfoundation.org/articles/69379/an-essay-on-criticism.

2. He actually won *two* Nobel Prizes: One was in chemistry and the other was the Peace Prize.

3. Megan Thielking, "How Linus Pauling Duped America into Believing Vitamin C Cures Colds," *Vox*, February 27, 2015, https://www.vox.com/2015/1/15/7547741/vitamin-c-myth-pauling.

4. More precisely, I will be using "knowledge" in the way philosophers have traditionally used it. For more on this, see "Introduction to Philosophy: 7.2 Knowledge," *OpenStax*, March 1, 2024, https://openstax.org/books/introduction-philosophy/pages/7-2-knowledge.

5. I am here making reference to Archbishop James Ussher's chronology of the events described in the Old Testament. There is, by the way, disagreement about whether creation took place on the 22nd or the 23rd.

6. Leo Tolstoy, *The Kingdom of God Is Within You*, trans. Constance Garnett (Cassell Publishing, 1894), 21, https://archive.org/details/TheKingdomOfGodIsWithinYou/.

7. This is from the "Economy" chapter of *Walden*.

8. Donald Rumsfeld, "Rumsfeld/Knowns," *CNN*, March 31, 2016, https://www.youtube.com/watch/REWeBzGuzCc.

9. This episode is described in Plato's *Apology*.

10. For an insightful study of willful ignorance, see Ralph Hertwig and Dagmar Ellerbrock, "Why People Choose Deliberate Ignorance in Times of Societal Transformation," *Cognition* 226 (December 2022): 105247, https://www.sciencedirect.com/science/article/pii/S0010027722002359.

Chapter 13

1. The World Wide Web is the system of interlinked hypertext documents on the internet that can be accessed with web browsers.
2. To dox people is to publicly identify or publish private information about them, which can include where they live and work, as well as information about their family members.
3. "The Birth of the Web," *CERN*, https://home.web.cern.ch/science/computing/birth-web.
4. Walter Isaacson, "Early Internet Directories—David Filo, Jerry Yang, and Yahoo!," November 29, 2020, https://www.youtube.com/watch/x_cfVUHp8PY.
5. In July 2024, a Google search for the word "the" returned 25,270,000,000 results.
6. Matthew Rosenberg, Nicholas Confessore, and Carole Cadwalledr, "How Trump Consultants Exploited the Facebook Data of Millions," *New York Times*, March 17, 2018, https://www.nytimes.com/2018/03/17/us/politics/cambridge-analytica-trump-campaign.html.
7. "Pure" Thinkers wouldn't be susceptible, but as we have seen, such beings don't exist.
8. James Vincent, "Twitter Is Bringing Its 'Read Before You Retweet' Prompt to All Users," *The Verge*, September 25, 2020, https://www.theverge.com/2020/9/25/21455635/twitter-read-before-you-tweet-article-prompt-rolling-out-globally-soon.
9. Kevin Roose, "What Is QAnon, the Viral Pro-Trump Conspiracy Theory?" *New York Times*, September 3, 2021, https://www.nytimes.com/article/what-is-qanon.html.

10. Farah Pandith and Jacob Ware, "Teen Terrorism Inspired by Social Media Is on the Rise. Here's What We Need to Do," *Think: Opinion, Analysis, Essay, NBC*, March 22, 2021, https://www.nbcnews.com/think/opinion/teen-terrorism-inspired-social-media-rise-here-s-what-we-ncna1261307.
11. Liv McMahon and Zoe Kleinman, "Glue Pizza and Eat Rocks: Google AI Search Errors Go Viral," *BBC*, May 24, 2024, https://www.bbc.com/news/articles/cd11gzejgz4o.
12. Ernest Hemingway is reputed to have written "For sale. Baby shoes. Never worn," to demonstrate just how short a story could be, but this attribution is contested. See David Haglund, "Did Hemingway Really Write His Famous Six-Word Story?" *Slate*, January 31, 2013, https://slate.com/culture/2013/01/for-sale-baby-shoes-never-worn-hemingway-probably-did-not-write-the-famous-six-word-story.html. And full disclosure: I subsequently asked Perplexity to write a *funny* fictional story that contains those sentences. The result was not as funny as the original story was sad.
13. AI mavens refer to this as the "dual-use problem."
14. Jess Craig, "Widely Available AI Could Have Deadly Consequences," *Wired*, May 17, 2022, https://www.wired.com/story/ai-dr-evil-drug-discovery/.
15. Nicholas Kristof, "A.I. May Save Us or May Construct Viruses to Kill Us," *New York Times*, July 27, 2024, https://www.nytimes.com/2024/07/27/opinion/ai-advances-risks.html.
16. "Video: Geoffrey Hinton Talks About the 'Existential Threat' of AI," 21:40, *MIT Technology Review*, May 3, 2023, https://www.technologyreview.com/2023/05/03/1072589/video-geoffrey-hinton-google-ai-risk-ethics.
17. Although a Thinker won't outsource her thinking to AI—and let it tell her what to think—she might employ AI platforms as research tools, the way she employs conventional search engines as research tools.

Chapter 14

1. At the time of this writing, Kagi.com was one such engine. DuckDuckGo.com didn't sell users' data, but it did show them ads.
2. The networks in question were ABC, CBS, NBC, and, starting in 1975, PBS.
3. Phil Corbett, "Why Does The New York Times Use Anonymous Sources?" *New York Times*, June 30, 2022, https://www.nytimes.com/article/why-new-york-times-anonymous-sources.html.
4. It is a reasonable thing to hope for. *The New York Times* started its online edition in 1996. By 2024, only 6 percent of its subscribers still received the print edition. See Benjamin Mullin, "New York Times Adds 210,000 Digital Subscribers in Quarter," *New York Times*, May 8, 2024, https://www.nytimes.com/2024/05/08/business/media/new-york-times-earnings.html.
5. At the time of this writing, Snopes.com and PolitiFact.com were two such sites.

Chapter 15

1. John Stuart Mill, *On Liberty* (Hackett, 1978), 34.
2. Mill, *On Liberty*, 35.
3. Realize that it will take thought and effort to find these podcasts because for every Thinker podcast there might be a hundred Feeler podcasts.
4. Mill, *On Liberty*, 35.

Chapter 16

1. At the time of this writing, the Allsides.com aggregator attempts to do this.

Chapter 17

1. You might occasionally feel too tired to think, the way you occasionally feel too tired to exercise. Also, as we have seen, your heart and gut might incapacitate your thought processes.

2. Plato, *Gorgias*, trans. W. R. M. Lamb (Harvard University Press, 1925), 458a.
3. "The Curious Mr. Feynman," *Freakonomics* (podcast), January 31, 2024, https://freakonomics.com/podcast/the-curious-mr-feynman/.
4. Richard P. Feynman, "Cargo Cult Science," *Engineering and Science* 37, no. 7 (June 1974): 12, https://calteches.library.caltech.edu/51/2/CargoCult.pdf.

Chapter 18

1. Some possible alternatives: Should the Elgin marbles be returned to Greece? Was COVID-19 the result of a lab leak? Should single-use plastic be banned? Should colleges and universities have sports teams?

INDEX

For the benefit of digital users, indexed terms that span two pages (e.g., 52–53) may, on occasion, appear on only one of those pages.

abortion debate, use of emotive
　　language in, 90
absolutism
　　consequences of, 60–61
　　with respect to pacifism, 59–60
agnosticism
　　deliberate, 23
　　naïve, 23
AI. *See* artificial intelligence
ambiguity
　　characterized, 77–78
　　comedic use of, 78–79
　　commercial use of, 79–80
　　communication problems
　　　　caused by, 78
　　source of friction in
　　　　relationships, 80
　　Thinker's response to, 85
ambiguous questions
　　regarding abortion, 81
　　regarding evolution, 82–83
　　regarding Islam, 82
　　regarding men's rudeness, 81
　　regarding poverty rate, 84–85
　　regarding UFOs, 82
　　regarding unemployment rate, 83–84
anonymity
　　impact of, on people's
　　　　behavior, 183–84
　　provided by internet, 190
argufiers, 37–38
arguments. *See also* debates
　　value of, xi
　　winning, 37
Armstrong, Karen, 79–80
artificial intelligence (AI)
　　dangers posed by, 195–96
　　difficult to rein in, 196–97
　　history of, 194–95
　　presence of, makes it harder
　　　　to stay grounded in
　　　　reality, 195–96
　　presence of, makes us susceptible
　　　　to manipulation, 196
　　Thinker's response to, 197
astrology, 50–51
Aurelius, Marcus, 155
author (of this book)
　　classroom experience of, 1,
　　　　64, 91–92
　　role as thinking coach, xi–xii
　　shortcomings of, x

belief. *See also* disbelief; nonbelief;
  contrasted with knowledge, 174–76
  examined, 1
  isn't binary, 25
  "seeds," 161, 162, 242
beliefs, acquisition of
  based on direct experience, 29
  based on fast thinking, 215
  based on memory, 30–31
  based on physical evidence, 29–30
  from other people, 34–36
beliefs, categorized
  black and white, 26–27
  conscious and unconscious, 32
  empty, 18–19
  fuzzy, 19–20
  gray, 26–27
  hot and cold, 27–28
  popular, 214–15
beliefs, confidence level in
  certainty is rarely possible, 213–14
  depends on many factors, 23–25
  dimmer switch analogy, 25
beliefs, inconsistent
  characterized, 55–56
  difficult to detect, 73
  easy to acquire, 73
  examples of, 56–57
  psychological irritation caused by, 73–74
beliefs, inferred, 31–32, 33
beliefs, inherited, 34, 213
beliefs, mistaken
  acting on, 17–18, 26
  are skilled imposters, 17, 25–26
  easy to hold, 17–18
beliefs, religious
  often "inherited," 94–95
  should be chosen with care, 95–97

belief set
  presence of unconscious beliefs in, 33–34
  size of, 33–34
bias. *See* cognitive biases; confirmation bias
Bigfoot, 24, 47–48, 56
blind spots, the importance of finding and eliminating, 222–23
Boris (fictional character), 183–85, 192
brain
  structure of, 1–2
  "wiring" of, 2
brainstorming, 131
broilers, 62–64
bubbles. *See* filter bubbles
budgeting your thought, 51–52, 165
burden-of-proof principle
  applied to internet, 53
  applied to religion, 52–53
  explained, 51
  shifting the burden of proof, 52
butterfly effect, 111

campaigns, political, 139
category mistakes
  characterized, 102–3
  harm done by, 103–4
  made with respect to meaning of life, 105–6
"cats sit," meaning of, 77–78
causal explanations, 113–14
causal fallacies
  characterized, 112–13
  involving post hoc reasoning, 112–13
causation
  backward, 114–15
  coincidental, 113–14

complexity of, 109–10
confounding factors in, 113
experiments to establish, 114–17
reciprocal, 113
using time travel to establish, 115
causation, understanding of
improves ability to predict the
future, 119–20
will be a goal of Thinkers, 120
certainty, feelings of
rarely justified, 23–24
why we seek them, 25–26
chickens. *See* broilers; cockfighting
circumcision, 92–93, 94
claims
complex, 41–42
involving statistical
generalizations, 44–45
involving universal
generalizations, 42–44
simple, 41
claims of necessity
are a special kind of universal
generalization, 46
can be refuted with stories, 45–46
characterized, 45
contrasted with claims of fact, 45
made by absolutists, 59–60
cockfighting, 61–64
cognitive biases. *See also* confirmation
bias; Dunning–Kruger effect
characterized, 2, 160
examples of, 160–61
how mankind acquired, 2, 159–60
with respect to ideologies, 166–67
cognitive dissonance, 73–74
common sense, 203
confirmation bias
avoidance of, 164–66
characterized, x, 161

experienced by voters, 161
pervasiveness of, 162–64
with respect to false claims, 162
with respect to ideologies, 166–67
conspiracy theories
advocates of, 125
appeal of, 124–25
Pizzagate, 189–90
Thinker's response to, 125
contradictory beliefs
blatant, 61
latent, 61
people's unwillingness to admit
holding, xii
control group (in an experiment), 115
correlations
are different than "links," 113–14
coincidental, 113–14
counterexamples
can take the form of stories, 46
characterized, 43–44
COVID-19, 111–12
creeping expertise, 173–74
critical thinking
complements open-mindedness, 5
involves evidence-based systematic
thinking, 6–7
crowds, wisdom of
examples of, 39
reliance of Thinkers on, 39–40

"dead dogma," 217
debates
downside of, xi, 37
participation in, by argufiers, 37–38
role of, in belief formation, 37–38
as a source of ego gratification, xi
decision-making
accounting for contingencies as
part of, 145

decision-making (*cont.*)
  accounting for personal values as part of, 146
  anxiety experienced during, 148, 152
  on "autopilot," 143–44
  can involve problem-solving, 143–44
  Feeler's approach to, 147–49
  impact of, on future well-being, 149, 152
  involves pros-and-cons reasoning, 145–47, 148
  procrastination in, 147, 152
  shortcuts for, 151–55
  systematic approach to, 145–47
  Thinker's approach to, 146–47, 152
decisions
  assessing quality of, 149–50, 151–52
  beneficial (as opposed to prudent), 149–51
  conscious and unconscious, 143–44
  made routinely, 143–44
  prudent (as opposed to beneficial), 149–51
"deepities," 101–2
Dennett, Daniel, 79–80, 101–2
disbelief. *See also* belief; nonbelief
  characterized, 21
discrimination
  ambiguity of the word, 90–92
  on the basis of gender, 169
  in the classroom, 90–91
  emotional impact of the word, 91–92
divine providence, theory of
  described, 50
  is not falsifiable, 50
double standards
  characterized, 68
  how they arise, 71–72

Dunning–Kruger effect, 171–72

economics of thinking, 51–52
effects (psychological)
  backfire, 160, 179
  rhyme-as-reason, 161
ego
  affects what we believe, 73
  blinds us to our mistakes, 233
  is concerned with our public image, xii
Emerson, Ralph Waldo, 57–58
emotions
  can be triggered by choice of words, 90
  desirability of, xiii
  impact of, on reasoning ability, xiii
  impossible to eliminate, xi
  things that trigger, ix–x, 2, 27–28
  Thinker does not attempt to extinguish, 7
events
  can be difficult to predict, 111
  have multiple causal factors, 109–10
existential claims
  characterized, 46–47
  harder to disprove than to prove, 47
experiments
  controlled, 115, 118
  double-blind, 118
  must take account of placebo effect, 115–16
  natural, 119
  that violate human rights, 118–19
experts
  reliability of, 38
  Thinkers' reliance on, 39
eyewitness testimony, 30–31

Fairness Doctrine, 206–7

fallacies
  anecdotal, 160
  gambler, 160
  planning, 160
falsifiability, 49–50, 214
Feelers. *See also* intellectual spectrum; Thinkers
  beliefs of, will differ from those of Thinkers, 124–25
  can be "pure," 123
  characterized, 121–22, 123
  existence of, 122
  intellectual inflexibility of, 230–31
  often difficult to reason with, 122
  will be attracted to conspiracy theories, 125
feminism, 167–69
Feynman, Richard, 232–33
filter bubbles
  characterized, 188–89
  consequences of residing in, 188–89
  impact of, on democracy, 193
  impact of, on dispute resolution, 193
  impact of, on people's perception of reality, 193
  resulting from repeal of Fairness Doctrine, 206–7
  role of internet in formation of, 188
  Thinkers are not immune to, 188–89
fitness
  mental, ix
  physical, ix

gatekeepers
  internet, 184
  traditional, 183
generalizations, statistical
  can't be disproved with counterexamples, 44–45
  examples of, 44

generalizations, sweeping
  are more likely to be made by Feelers, 124
  can give rise to inconsistent beliefs, 71
generalizations, universal
  can be disproved with counterexamples, 43–44
  forms they can take, 42–43
  harder to prove than to disprove, 43–44
genital mutilation. *See* circumcision
God
  belief in, 18–19, 23
  concept and history of, 79–80
gut
  in conflict with head, 1–2
  as source of beliefs, 28

head
  in conflict with heart and gut, 1–2
  as source of beliefs, 28
heart
  in conflict with head, 1–2
  as source of beliefs, 28
hijacking of head by heart and gut, 2, 7
Hinton, Geoffrey, 105, 197
Hirdt, Steve, 113–14
history
  importance of studying, 132–33, 228
  lesson of, 132–33
Hitler, Adolph, 111
horse, story of runaway, 151
human factor, 111–12
hypocrisy, 57

ideologies
  danger of being taken captive by, 167
  examples of, 166
  value of, 166–67

ignorance
  admission of, xii
  characterized, 177
  contrasted with being misinformed, 177
  contrasted with being stupid, 179
ignorance, willful. *See also* blind spots
  can give rise to inconsistencies, 70, 180
  can have tragic consequences, 180
  characterized, 179–80
  using mind expansion regimen to overcome, 222–23
inconsistency
  blatant and latent, 56, 61
  "developing" latent, 64–65
  distinguished from hypocrisy, 57
  synchronous and asynchronous, 57–58
  Thinker's response to, 58–59
  ways to resolve, 56–57
  why we harbor, 71–74
inflation, 111–12
intellectual spectrum. *See also* Feelers; Thinkers
  characterized, 122–23
  endpoints of, 122–23
  people usually fall in the middle of, 122–23
internet. *See also* search engines; social media platforms
  appearance of "rabbit holes" on, 189–90
  dark side of, 189
  gullibility of users, 190–91
  has been a mixed blessing for Thinkers, 193
  has polluted the information space, 191
  history of, 185–86
  impact of, on journalism, 207–8
  launch of World Wide Web (WWW), 184, 185–86
  political impact of, 186–87
  provides a cloak of anonymity, 190
  provides a "megaphone" for reaching the masses, 190
  searches on, 187–88
  targeted advertising on, 186–87
  tribe formation on, 192–93
  website creation on, 189
irrational people, xiii–xiv

Johnson, Lyndon, 139

Kahneman, Daniel, 2, 160
know-it-alls, 172–73
knowledge
  characterized, 174–75
  contrasted with belief, 174–76
  contrasted with intelligence, 176
  contrasted with wisdom, 176
  sought by Thinkers, 176
  of what we don't know, 177–78

labels, binary, 27
language, emotive
  can disrupt thought processes, 90–92
  examples of, 89–90
legality, distinguished from morality, 81
life, meaning of, 105–6
limbic system, 1–2
linguistic pitfalls, 99, 102, 106
love, claims regarding, 101

masculinism (or masculism)
  characterized, 167–68
  debate regarding, 167–69
MegaSyn (AI platform), 195
memory
  malleability of, 30
  trustworthiness of, 30–31

metaphors
  proper use of, 105
  use of, in the Bible, 104–5
metathinking (or metacognition), 234
Mill, John Stuart, 217–18
mindcare regimen. *See also* mindcleaning regimen; mind-expansion regimen
  characterized, 201, 202
  choosing news sources, 205–9
  relying on AI search engines for information, 204–5
  relying on internet for information, 203
  relying on other people for information, 203
  relying on traditional search engines for information, 203–4
  role of "shoe-leather journalism" in, 221–22
mindcleaning regimen. *See also* mindcare regimen; mind-expansion regimen
  characterized, 201, 211
  mindcleaning priorities, 212–15
  mindcleaning strategies, 211–12
mind-expansion regimen. *See also* mindcare regimen; mindcleaning regimen
  broadened exposure to news sources, 221–22
  characterized, 201
  exploration of Feelers' minds, 225
  exposure to iconoclastic Thinkers, 224–25
  finding and dealing with blind spots, 222–23
  geographical and intellectual exploration of the world, 224
  justification for, 201–2
  seeing things from different perspectives, 222–24
mind optimization
  characterized, x–xi, 4–5
  emotional challenges to, xiii
  impossibility of achieving perfection, xiii
  journey toward, xiii, 242
  justification for, 4
  mental challenges of, xiii
  obstacles to, xi–xii
  program for, 201
  requires critical thinking, 5
  requires open-mindedness, 4, 5
morality, distinguished from legality, 81
"mysterious stranger" story
  described, 64–68
  possible responses to, 68–70
  student response to, 71

news aggregators, 208
news environment
  impact of cable television on, 206–7
  impact of internet on, 207–8
Nixon, Richard, 140
no-knock laws, 140–41
nonbelief. *See also* belief; disbelief
  aversion to, 21–22
  characterized, 21
  deliberate, 22–23
  naïve, 22–23

open-minded critical thinking
  exercises involving, 235–37
  impact of, on self, xiv
  impact of, on society, xiv
  often isn't taught in college, 35–36
  Thinker excels in, 5
open-mindedness
  characterized, x–xi
  complements critical thinking, 5

overthinking, 234
ozone hole, 119–20

pacifism, absolute
   challenged with a story, 59–60
   characterized, 59–60
pacifism, generic, 59
Pauling, Linus, 173–74
"pebble-in-shoe" phenomenon, 74
Pizzagate conspiracy theory, 189–90
placebo effect, 115–16
polymath, 172–73
poverty rate, different
     characterizations of, 84–85
predictions
   self-defeating, 111–12
   self-fulfilling, 111–12
   Thinker will be guarded in
     making, 121
   Thinker will be wary of those made
     by others, 120–21
   tricks played by prognosticators, 120
predictive processing, 32
prefrontal cortex, 1–2
Princip, Gavrilo, 109, 110
problems
   analysis of, 129–31
   characterized, 127
   Feeler's response to, 128
   personal, 138
   sorting, 128
   Thinker's response to, 128–29
   tree-like structure of, 130–31
   ubiquity of, 127, 128
problems, societal
   characterized, 129–30, 138–39
   how dealt with in a democracy,
     138–39, 141
   solutions to, can give rise to new
     problems, 140–41
   solutions to, can make things
     worse, 140
   war on drugs, 140–41
   war on poverty, 139–40
problem-solving
   assessing consequences, 132
   assessing costs, 131–32
   assessing solutions, 136–38
   can require decision-
     making, 143–44
   Feeler's approach to, 135–36
   finding optimal solutions,
     133–36
   listing possible solutions, 131
   role of brainstorming in, 131
   systematic approach to, 131–38
   tradeoffs involved in, 133–35
proof, conclusive, 41
proving negatives, 47
proving nonexistence, 47–48
psychology
   cognitive, 2
   evolutionary, 1–2
   value of studying, 1, 119–20
puns, 78–79

QAnon conspiracy theory, 184

racial and racist claims, 92
"racism," ambiguity of, 86–87
rationalization
   characterized, 2
   contrasted with reasoning, 73
reality
   being grounded in, 3, 4
   deniers, 3–4
   is inanimate, 4
   is terrible at keeping secrets, 4
   nature of, 3–4
   objective, 3–4

perception of, has been fragmented
by internet, 193, 195–96
personal, 3
roles for living, 154–55
rules for living, 153–54
Russell, Bertrand, 28
Ryle, Gilbert, 103

scientific studies, 229–30
scientists
   capable of feeling their way to
      conclusions, ix, 116–17
   capable of thinking better, x
   capable of thinking more, ix–x
search engines, traditional
   are being supplanted by AI
      searches, 194
   business model behind, 186
   customized results of, 187–88
   inception of, 186
   mechanism of, 186
sensitivity to initial conditions. *See*
   butterfly effect
sham surgery, 116
"shoe-leather journalism," 205–6
shortcuts, cognitive, 2
social media platforms
   impact of, on human behavior, 185
   inception of, 185
   source of disinformation, 189
socialism, 19–20
Socrates, 7–8, 178–79, 232
Stoicism, 155
stories
   used to refute absolute
      pacifists, 59–60
   used to refute claims of
      necessity, 45–46
stress testing of beliefs
   absent from many classrooms, 217–18
   process for, 215–17
   results of, 217, 218–19
   role of "contrary Thinker" in,
      215–16, 217
   substitutes for, 215–16, 217–18
stupidity, 179
surrogate thinkers
   characterized, 36
   confidence level of, 36
   use of, by Thinkers, 38, 39
Sykes, Brian, 48

talk radio, 206–7
test group (in an experiment), 115
theories, scientific
   characterized, 48–49
   distinguished from commonplace
      theories, 82–83
   falsifiability of, 49–50
Thinkers. *See also* Feelers; intellectual
   spectrum
   approach of, to decision-
      making, 146–47
   approach of, to problem-
      solving, 128–29
   becoming one, 6–7, 227, 233–
      34, 237–38
   beliefs of, will differ from those of
      Feelers, 124–25
   can disagree with other
      Thinkers, 8–9
   characterized, 5–7, 9, 123–
      24, 227–28
   epistemic humility of, 173, 177–
      78, 230
   exercises for prospective, 235–37
   gender of, 5
   independent-mindedness
      of, 231–32
   intellectual flexibility of, 230–31

Thinkers (*cont.*)
  interest of, in history, 132–33, 228
  interest of, in science, 119–20, 228
  misconceptions regarding, 6–8, 9
  news sources favored by, 208–9
  reliance of, on crowds, 39–40
  reliance of, on experts, 39
  response of, to complexity, 231
  response of, to conspiracy theories, 125
  response of, to criticism, 232
  response of, to uncertainty, 230
  skepticism of, 229–30
  views of, regarding ideologies, 167, 169
  will be slow to form opinions, 228–29
  will engage in mindful thinking, 234
  will not be "pure," 123
thinking
  affected by ego, xii
  better, ix
  more, ix–x
  obstacles to, xi–xii
  about politics, ix–x
  about science, ix–x
  selective, ix
thought regimens. *See also* mindcare regimen; mindcleaning regimen; mind-expansion regimen
  goal of, x–xi
thoughtful discussion, xi
time-frame problem, in decision-making, 151
time travel, used to establish causation, 115
Tolstoy, Leo, 177
tribes
  attraction of, for Feelers, 192
  avoidance of, by Thinkers, 192
  formation of, 191–92
  internet, 192–93
  members of, can form mobs, 192
  members of, can hold extremist views, 192–93
Tversky, Amos, 2, 160

unemployment, alternative definitions of, 83–84

values, personal, 146

war on drugs, 140–41
war on poverty, 139–40
Welch, Edgar Maddison, 189–90
wisdom, 176
witchcraft, 39–40
word definitions
  correctness of, 87
  lexical, 87
  stipulative, 87
  Thinker's views regarding, 87–88
words
  invention of new, 86, 87
  repurposing of old, 86–87
  using them contrasted with mentioning them, 100–2

zero-sum bias, 160